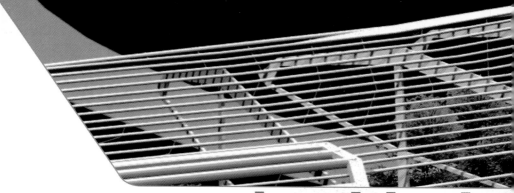

ivor richards

GROUNDSCRAPERS + SUBSCRAPERS
of hamzah & yeang

WILEY-ACADEMY

First published in Great Britain in 2001 by Wiley Academy

A division of
John Wiley & Sons
Baffins Lane
Chichester
West Sussex P019 1UD

ISBN 0-470-84354-3

Other Wiley Editorial offices
New York • Weinheim • Brisbane • Singapore • Toronto

Printed and bound in Malaysia by EHT Creative & Graphic Services

Book Credits (refer to last page)

for Sarah and Owen

would like to record my gratitude to Ken Yeang for his help in assembling all
e research material, and also to his colleagues Ridzwa Fathan, Yenniu Lim
nd Lucy Chew in the process and production of the text and layouts.
qually, I would like to thank my colleagues Stuart Cameron, Simon Guy
nd Norman Harper, at Newcastle University, for enabling the project in
rious ways.

nally, I should express my thanks to Maggie Toy and Wiley Academy in
e realisation of the publication.

contents

content page

008-009
010-...
011-013

014-023
024-033
034-045
046-057
058-065
066-073
074-083
084-089
090-093
094-103
104-109
110-117

marsham street urban design 2.16
bishopsgate 2.18

WIPO 2.13

al-asima 2.19
al-hilali 2.22

jabal omar 2.21

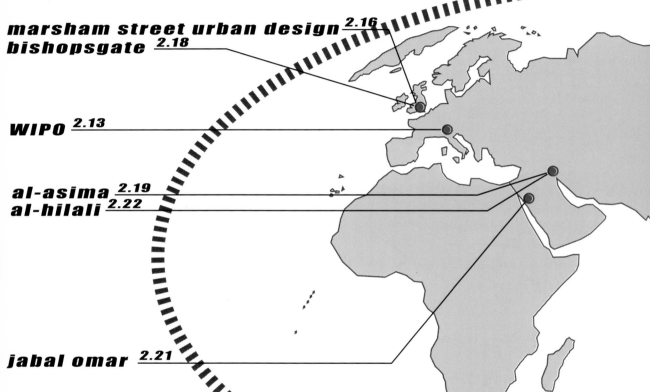

locations

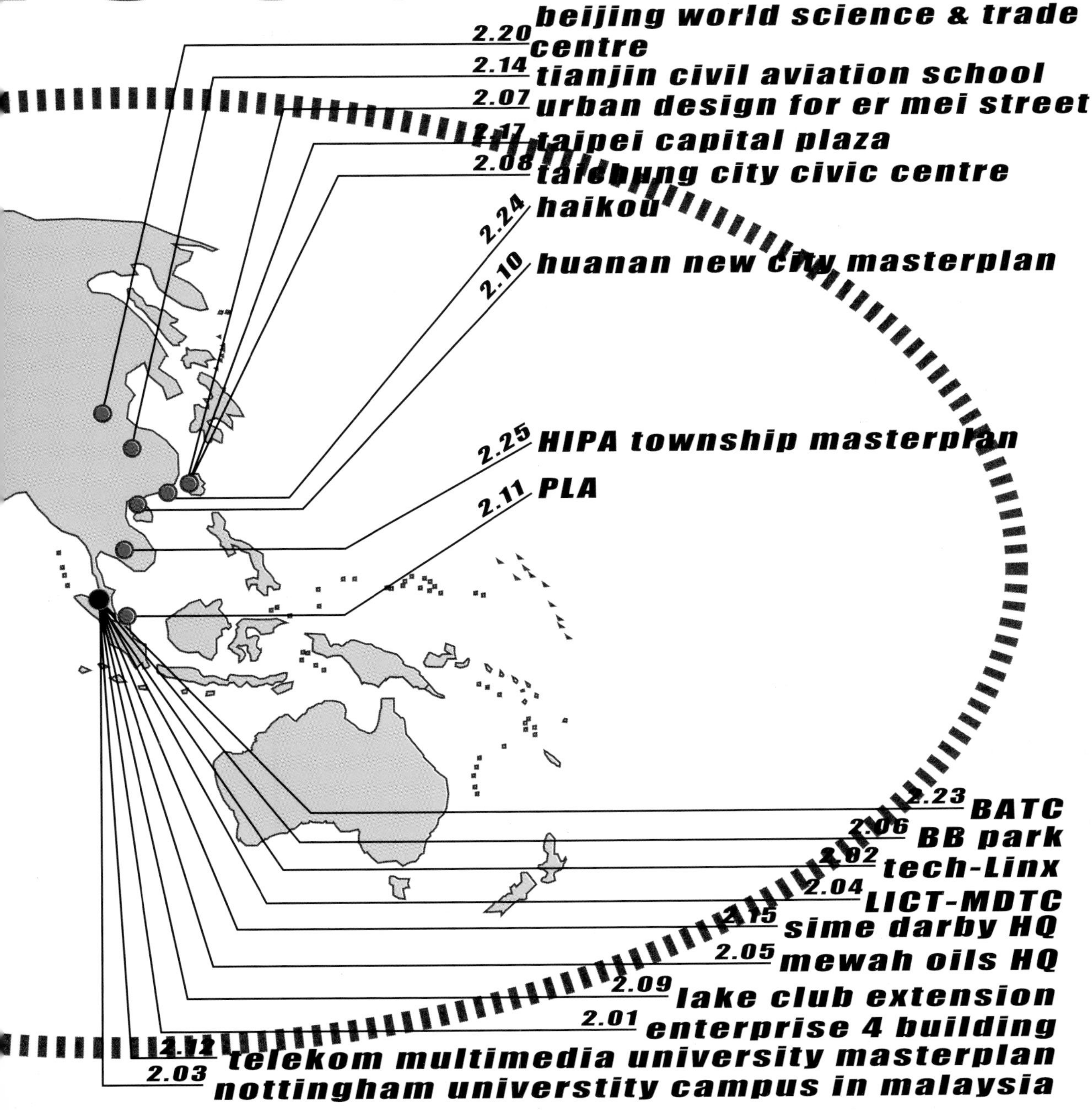

2.20 beijing world science & trade centre

2.14 tianjin civil aviation school

2.07 urban design for er mei street

2.17 taipei capital plaza

2.08 taichung city civic centre

2.24 haikou

2.10 huanan new city masterplan

2.25 HIPA township masterplan

2.11 PLA

2.23 BATC

2.06 BB park

2.02 tech-Linx

2.04 LICT-MDTC

2.15 sime darby HQ

2.05 mewah oils HQ

2.09 lake club extension

2.01 enterprise 4 building

2.12 telekom multimedia university masterplan

2.03 nottingham universtity campus in malaysia

Hovering above or contained within the ground-plane the architecture of groundscraper or subscraper defines new formal typologies. Ken Yeang's vision of his firm Hamzah & Yeang groundscraper and subscraper series is that of a skyscraper in a horizontal mode. That is the green skyscraper with its vertical urbanism rotated through 90 degrees. The significance of the groundscraper, as Yeang's notes on design indicate, is its great scale of footprint and impact on location-ecosystem. This determines a preferred builtform of lin-

1.3 notes on groundscraper + subscraper design

ken yeang

Groundscrapers and subscrapers are the antithesis of skyscrapers. These are the low and medium-rise buildings that devour the ground plane, spreading laterally outwards as a single large-sprawling built-form, or as clusters and mats of built-forms. In contrast to the skyscraper's morphology that extends vertically sky-wards, these extend horizontally and laterally across the ground plane and below.

Their first obvious characteristic is their large foot-print on the ground plane which can significantly alter the natural systems of the ecosystem that they are located. By comparison, the groundscraper and subscraper have by far a much more wide-spread foot-print (in terms of ground-coverage or 'plinth-ratio') than the skyscraper. The skyscraper is after all essentially a tall building with a relatively small or "postage-stamp" foot-print in relation to its vertical mass. The ratio of the skyscraper's foot-print to it's height would be significantly greater than 1:3, whereas the ground-scraper's ratio of maximum girth to height would in most instances be of a negative value.

This considerably larger horizontal mass and foot-print will in most instances have a greater physical presence and environmental impact on the location's ecosystem and its systemic functioning. Particularly in the case of green-field sites, (regardless of whether the land here is covered with diverse vegetation or a mono-culture agricultural field), the land will for instance, usually have edaphic factors such as a top-soil that is rich with nutrients and

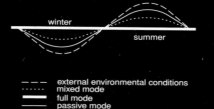

• Like the prosthetic device, the man-made built environment must interface integrally with the organic ecosystem.

• Design must all passive mode strategies before adopting mixed-mode and full mode strategies.

• The biosphere is increasingly saturated with the man-made environment. Ecological design must seek to reverse this trend.

winter / summer

- - - external environmental conditions
······ mixed mode
—— full mode
passive mode

ecological environment — artificial environment

ecological environment → artificial environment

ecosystems — artificial environment

ecosystems → ecosystem

The Biosphere - Stage 1

The Biosphere - Stage

ar extensions or clusters interspersed with continuous landscape. The new linear or cluster typologies occur through the evolution of Hamzah & Yeang's architecture from bioclimatic to ecological design. The resultant architecture could not be ... > >>

complex micro-organic life being integral with that ecosystem's flora and fauna.

Once this rich top-soil layer has been scraped away (and worse, wasted by not being re-used elsewhere) by construction activity and then subsequently resurfaced with tarmac or concrete or some impervious construction, that micro-organic life in this ground cover is lost for any future re-vegetation or for arable use. Furthermore, the opportunity for rain-fall to infiltrate through the ground to return into the ground-water will also be inhibited, and over the long term the locality's hydrological regime will be affected which will subsequently influence the other ecological factors of the locality.

In master planning, the site layout's design should at the onset seek to avoid laying out large areas of impervious surfaces over the ground plane. Whether in designing or masterplanning the groundscraper or the subscraper, the layout pattern should preferably be one of a series of green 'fingers' or linked linear 'patches' of green vegetated-strips, in which the synthetic impervious builtform components are non-continuous and wedged in-between the continuously-vegetated organic mass (e.g. see Nottingham University Masterplan).

We might contend here that a crucial aspect in the design of groundscrapers and subscrapers, is the provision by design of linked or continuously vegetated-planting zones as **'ecological corridors'**. These are the biologically important zones that contribute to maintaining (and even improving) the biodiversity of the locality by enabling the various species of flora and fauna to migrate and to interact with each other as well as with the other ecological factors of the locality. By enabling and enhancing these ecosystem functions by design, a layout pattern with ecological corridors will tend to engender a more diverse and eventually a more stable ecosystem that will have greater survival potential. Wherever such organic linkages are non-existent or have been physically interrupted, our new master plan's design should introduce or facilitate such linkages. Generally stated, our masterplan's design should recreate in the plan new connected corridors of sustainably-managed, protected land zones, as vital 'ecological corridors'.

We can illustrate the importance of such 'ecological corridors' in a natural phenomenon that happened in the American continent, about sixty million years ago. The two Americas continents had collided in what plate-tectonic scientists call a 'pivotal natural event' in the earth's recent geological history. The impact of this collision resulted in creating a new biological corridor that links the North and South Americas together. This corridor's consequences on the biome were profound. At this point in the earth's ecological history, everything then changed – ocean currents, climate and the distribution of plants and animals on land, air and sea. This new ecological 'corridor of life' enabled for the first time the multitude of flora and fauna species from the two continents to migrate, interact and mix and resulted in a zone of rich and high biodiversity, all located there at this narrow isthmus that joins the North and South Americas together. Clearly when carrying out masterplanning design, if there is an existent ecological corridor in the locality, then this should be retained. Where such an ecological corridor is not existent, then new corridors might be introduced into the masterplan (and where possible) at locations that would best benefit the ecosystem.

Groundplane relationship of built forms are crucial to integrating man-made with the landscape.

The continuity of the landscape is vital for the enhancement of biodiversity.

Cross ventilation & wind flow can become key factors in site planning.

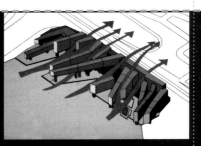

Where possible, this linked ecological corridor might be further integrated with the builtform by extending the vegetated landscape over the builtform itself and if possible also into and within the building as a form of horizontal and vertical integrated landscaping that should ideally be systemically integral with the inorganic components of the builtform. This design endeavour becomes one of the creation of new ecological habitats, which has previously been non-existent.

This introduction and increase in new organic mass into the new built environment will have several environmental benefits. Firstly it recreates new natural habitats within a biosphere which is now increasingly becoming artificial and man-made. This re-vegetation increase the organic mass in the built environment. The inclusion of more organic mass is beneficial to the location's macro-climate as it reduces the overall urban heat-island effect on that locality (if in an existent dense city context). Finally, the increase in planted material also improves the micro-climate, by its production of oxygen (through plant photosynthesis) and by the plants absorbing carbon dioxide and carbon monoxide.

A novel device that we might use in designing groundscraper and subscraper schemes is the 'landscaped bridge' concept (© Yeang, 2001). The landscaped bridge is essentially a well vegetated-platform that spans over an otherwise inorganic area (such as an impervious road or a high-way or some paved surfaces). The landscaped bridge is organically planted over and by its bridging function, ecologically links the vegetation between the two sides of the bridge.

The theoretical proposition here is that the two previously disparate vegetated zones will now become joined together through this wide vegetated bridge. The new green-bridge will also provide a new overhead ecological corridor that would enable flora and faunal species migration across the bridge thereby positively contributing (by design) to improving and enhancing the increase in the biodiversity of the locality. In such circumstances, our design endeavours would no longer become a receding battle of our designing to ensure minimal impacts on the ecosystems. It recognizes that by appropriate design, we can actually contribute positively to the biosphere's ecosystems by enabling the increase in the biodiversity of the locality.

The inverse adaptation of this bridge concept is of course, the 'landscaped underpass', which is an underground vegetated-underpass that in a similar way to the bridge can link two previously disparate green zones together (see Taipei).

The Dutch term for the 'skyscraper' literally translated refers to it as a building that 'gently touches the sky'. This is a much more benign description of the skyscraper and it's physical and visual impact on the skyline. By reverse analogy the groundscraper should be a building that touches the ground gently rather than scraping it, as the term 'groundscraper' might otherwise imply.

It is this physical impact on the ecosystem's ground plane by the cutting, altering or excavating of the earth that attention should be critically given when designing large spread-out buildings. This is not to mean that all earthworks have negative ecosystem impacts, but all earthworks inevitably involve the removal of ground cover and top-soil and the alteration of the site's topography

● We need to establish the limitations to which we can affect the environment.

● Sites need to be studied as ecosystems before permitting any man-made interference on it.

● Ecologically sensitive sites need to require a thorough study of the ecosystem in which they are located.

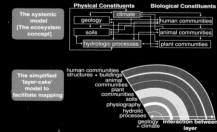

logical design. Ecological principles as applied to ar-
ment, nor is it concerned with temporary fashion rath-
order to understand Yeang's architecture, it is ... > >>

110

(whether to a greater or lesser extent) and the natural drainage routes. If this is not well considered by design, such action on the site's terrain can radically affect the locality's natural drainage, clear and destroy all the existent vegetation (and related fauna), lower the hydrological regime and ground-water tables, and subsequently lead to siltation of the surrounding waterways and other secondary effects.

A further extension of the groundscraper idea is the subscraper. Here, the builtform lies either totally or partially submerged underground. However to replace the disturbed ground and soil as a consequence of excavation, we can compensate this with a new roof-scape that is totally re-vegetated thereby returning the excavated land surface back into a natural habitat or by creating a new one altogether where previously non-existent.

In the case of the skyscraper, the planning of its access roads and related motorways (if applicable) and the impact of the layouts of these would generally not play as important a role in its design perhaps except at the immediate ground plane to the builtform and in most instances are of minimal importance unless the overall development is large or requires difficult road interchange patterns or related access roads. Clearly, ecological design must also consider the transportation consequences of the design, and acknowledge the relationship of the builtform (whether a skyscraper or groundscraper or subscraper) with the traffic infrastructure of the locality. This is because any new intensification of landuse would in all instances have significant energy consumption impacts arising from increased transportation by the new development's users travelling to and from the new builtform.

The groundscraper or subscraper are also spread-out builtforms, and the layout of their access roads within and outside their builtforms have a more crucial role in their site planning design particularly in the provision of all the horizontal access-ways such as pedestrian access, service vehicle routes, visitors access and parking, fire-engine access (especially to service difficult parts of the builtform, etc.), etc. Their routing, built platform levels, access surface gradients, drainage, etc. have to relate to the site's existent topography, as their patterns can inhibit or facilitate the provision of pedestrian vehicular-free routes, or inhibit the continuous organic relationships with the vegetation and other aspects of site planning. Layout design should in particular avoid any undesirable cross-overs of the key existent ecological corridors within the site, avoid the location of new impervious surfaces on those parts of the site that are prone to flooding and erosion, take into consideration natural vegetation diversity, natural drainage channels, soil factors, etc.

These are all the complex and interconnected aspects of the site's ecosystem at the vegetation layer, soils layer and at the ground level that are particularly important when designing groundscrapers and subscrapers. At the onset, a slope analysis and drainage analysis of the site's existent topography and the integration of the site's existent topography and ecological features with the new builtform and its access patterns are crucial in the ecological design and planning of the new groundscraper's and the subscraper's pattern of builtform.

Similar attention must be also given to the pattern of the new pedestrian networks, the placement of new large areas of impervious

The ecologist's definition of the environment must be the basis for all site planning.

• Transportation energy is a key consideration in masterplanning.

• Ecological landuse planning techniques provides one method for understanding the carrying capacity of the ecosystem as the basis for planning.

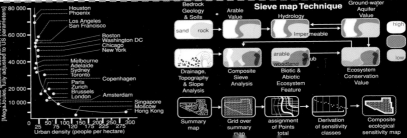

...sign must balance the abiotic components with ...biotic components in the man-made systems

surfaces (e.g. for car-parking or plazas), to the routing of all the infrastructural engineering systems (roads, drains, sewerage, water reticulation system, surface water drainage channels, telecommunications, night-lighting, waste disposal routes, etc.) to the creation of new earthworks platform levels, drainage routes, etc. Crucial to the overall approach in the ecological design and planning of groundscrapers and subscrapers is the use of the landscape architect's 'ecological landuse planning sieve-mapping technique' (based on the "layer-cake" model of the ecosystem). This approach to site analysis and masterplanning have been well developed by landscape architects in the 1960's (e.g. Ian Mcharg et al).

This method involves the mapping of the site's ecosystems through a system of map overlays and by means of cross-evaluations, it provides the ecological basis for site planning with the objective of making the least negative impacts (and at the same time endeavour to have the most positive impacts) on the site's ecology and its carrying capacity. The method enables the designer to locate with greater certainty all the new built structures, access roads and infrastructure systems in a way that minimizes any destructive impacts on the ecosystem's functioning and where possible, maximizes its environmental productivity.

Since groundscrapers are essentially medium-rise and low-rise builtforms, there are opportunities for linking groups of builtforms together with overhead large umbrella-like canopies. These can provide protection from the climate for pedestrians, to reduce solar heat-gain by shading the roof-space from direct sunlight in the summer, to make roofs useable for recreational use and for open-air functions, as well as providing semi-covered transitional spaces below and between buildings. This canopy need not in all instances be solid. It can be permeable or trellis-like with planting over, or it can be a retractable structure that can be open or shut depending on the use below and the season of the year.

The subscraper can also be an urban regeneration device for urban locations where the site has complex issues of multiple-ownerships of land titles thereby making redevelopment problematic, requiring lengthy negotiations and land acquisition. An example is the case of the urban regeneration of important parts of existing cities with a streetscape where the facades need to be retained. Often, one of the major inhibitors of regeneration is multiple land ownerships which require large-scale and exorbitant acquisition of properties.

A linear subscraper builtform provides the prototype solution where the entire land area occupied by the street itself (which is usually publicly-owned property) can become the zone for regeneration. The street has to be firstly made into a traffic-free zone. In order to retain the existing relationships between the existing buildings along the street, the design concept is to sink the entire new development underground as a linear groundscraper covering the extent (or part) of the length of the street itself between the building abutting the street. Inserted into the groundscraper could be large air-wells to bring day-light and natural ventilation into the enclosed and semi-enclosed spaces below ground.

Such linear subscraper builtforms as new developments built within the land occupied by the street, becomes a prototype for urban regeneration for those sites with similar streetscape conditions especially within the historic parts of existing cities. Here this becomes an alternative solution to the demolition of the existing buildings along an historically important street. The other proto-

• Masterplanning must also be based on the transportation patterns of their community.

• Ecological design equals an understanding of the complex interactions over the life-cycle of the built form.

• The landscaped bridge is a usual concept to enhance the locality's biodiversity and contribute positivity to the ecosystem.

Shopping education + religion

Bank

Services + personal business

24% 15%

5M 7.7M

33% 20%

10.6M 10.7M

work + related

Social, recreational + other

L22 Environment

L21 Inputs → L11 System → L12 Outputs

LP = L11 L12 / L21 L22

1   System
2   Environment to the system
L11 Processes + activities within the system
    [internal interdependences]
L22 Processes + activities in the environment of the system
    [external interdependences]
L12 Exchanges of the system with its environment
    [transactional interdependences of the system environment]
L21 Exchanges of the environment with the system
    [transactional interdependences of the environment system]
LP Ecological Design

rinciples of ecological or sustainable design. The
nvironmental assessment has been determined by
:kyscraper' (Prestel, Munich, 1999). In the . . . > >>

013

type groundscraper builtform typology is the wedge-shaped builtform or the 'wedgeform'. Here, the site's vegetation can start from the ground plane at the thin-end of the wedge and then work its way up along the wedge's roof to the thick-end of the wedge's builtform.

A corollary characteristic to the groundscraper's and subscraper's large foot-print is obviously their large roof-surfaces which can be vegetated and landscaped. This large roofscape provides an aerial 'camouflage' to the builtform. The enlarged roof area also provides design opportunities to thermally insulate the roof by vegetation. The roof plane can further provide useable areas for multi-use plazas by for example, enabling all-year usage of this space in temperate climatic zones through the use of retractable canopies to moderate the micro-climate depending on the season of the year. Design attention should also be paid to providing landscaping areas at not only the ground plane but also within the building itself through the generous provision of green sky-courts, elevated garden terraces and roof gardens, all of which can contribute to further enhancing the new builtform's eco-role as a new ecological habitat or mimetic ecosystem.

Another aspect to be considered in designing groundscrapers and subscrapers is their opportunities for improving urban connectivity. This may be crucial in the design of those sites with especially wide ground coverage. We might also use high-level bridges between builtforms and over the surrounding streets to improve such connectivities. As an alternative to the 'wedge-form' builtform, we can also mound the land forms at the sides of the builtform to create vegetated-mound-forms as another prototype typology to visually and physically blend the builtform horizontally with the ground plane and the landscape.

Ecological design generally stated, must seek a systemic harmonious relationship between the new man-made built-form and the ecological systems of the site within the context of the biosphere. To achieve this we might for example, increase or introduce new ecological connectivities that can be maintained through the use of "ecological corridors" or other similar landform devices such as 'land-bridges'. At the same time, our design should seek to balance the dense inorganicness and artificiality of the existent built-form with more new organic material to form new or extended ecological habitats. Most of our current man-made built-forms are usually artificial structures that are inserted or placed within the natural organic systems of that ecosystem where it is located. By analogy, these builtforms are like prosthesis (e.g. an artificial limbs) that have to integrate with the human body to which they are attached.

If it is an external prosthetic device then generally, its mechanical interface can be easily designed. In the case of an internal artificial organ, the tendency of the biological system (i.e. the human body) is to reject it as it would reject anything alien. The future of ecological design is therefore not only in the design of the built form as a large-scale prosthetic system, but more so in the design of its interface with the natural systems in the biosphere symbiotically. Being able to achieve a symbiosis between the artificial organ or prosthetic device with the biological or organic system in which it is inserted becomes the critical aspect of the future success of ecological design.

The basic patterns for interfacing organic mass (biotic components) with the inorganic in the built form.

● Masterplanning should take into account the thermal responses of the various ground surfaces.

● Biodiversity varies depending on the locality.

Horizontal Strategy

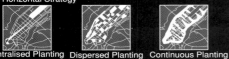

ntralised Planting　Dispersed Planting　Continuous Planting

Vertical Strategy

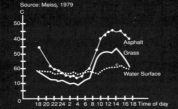

Source: Meiss, 1979

Asphalt
Grass
Water Surface

18 20 22 24 2 4 6 8 10 12 14 16 18 Time of day

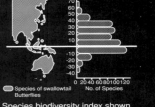

Latitude
70
60
50
40
30
20
10
-10
-20
-30
-40

0 20 40 60 80 100 120 No. of Species

Species of swallowtail Butterflies

Species biodiversity index shown in relation to latitude

enterprise 4

4+1basementno.sofstoreys 21 723sq.mSit

building

2.14 2.15 2.16 2.17 2.18 2.19 2.20   2.21   2.22.23 2.24 2.25

3.1 3.2   3.3   credits

Cyberjaya,Malaysia Location — **Project Data** —

2.45°N Latitude

1 870sq.m nett[excludingcarparks]:18 000sq.m carparkingprovision:600cars Areas Setia haruman Sdn. Bhd.Client 101.40 ELongitude

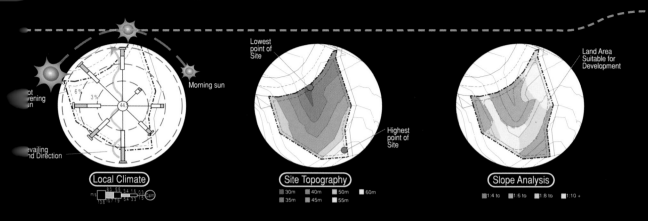

Local Climate

Morning sun
evening
un
evailing
nd Direction

6%   3%
44

Site Topography

Lowest point of Site
Highest point of Site

30m   40m   50m   60m
35m   45m   55m

Slope Analysis

Land Area Suitable for Development

1:4 to   1:6 to   1:8 to   1:10 +

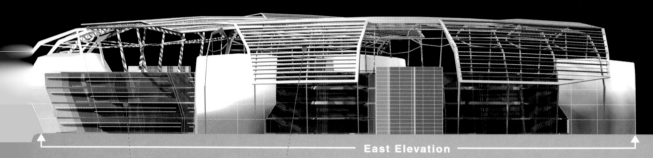

— **East Elevation** —

Enterprise Building 4 is a distinct type, situated in Yeang's low-rise architecture, that of unitary containers of space linked, unified and shielded by a hovering super-roof canopy structure. Sited in the   Enterprise Park Malaysia, with surrounding topography that includes a major high way, reservoir and steep terrain to the south, the four office-incubator units turn inward to a protected central courtyard garden. In turn the arrangement is served by a tree-lined peripheral driveway which gives access to each incubator. The figure of the court as a central organizing space, controlling the plan, is another characteristic of this type and shares a communality with some

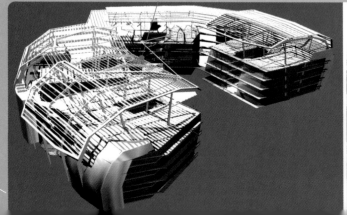

Study Model

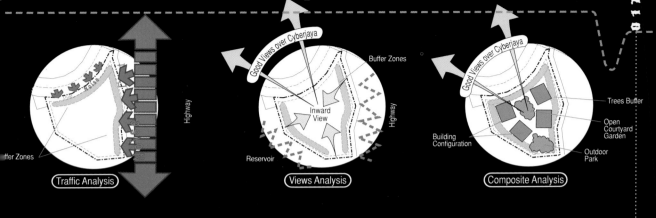

Traffic Analysis

Views Analysis

Composite Analysis

South Elevation

some of Yeang's ecological skyscraper series. Yeang has compared the appearance of the wrapped structure and louvered roof to that of an insect, which confirms its organic nature and form. The structure, roof and landscaped roof terraces both extend upwards from the ground, and provide a protective shell, shielding the overall form from the external site conditions and direct sunlight. The louvered structure, continuous over the roof gardens and paved terraces, is essentially a hovering canopy encircling the building and covered in a metal mesh membrane. A lower metal mesh roof covers the pivotal centre of the plan.

View from Road
A Interchange

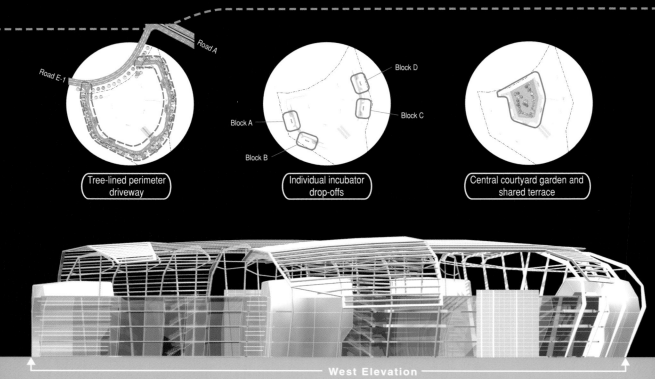

Road A

Road E-1

Block D

Block A

Block C

Block B

Tree-lined perimeter driveway

Individual incubator drop-offs

Central courtyard garden and shared terrace

West Elevation

These innovations in roof-shading forms provide 50% sunshading, which enables the roof terraces to be used for recreation, and at the same time to contribute to micro-environment cooling. In facilitating the roof-form in this way, Yeang's principles also open up the possibility of a major sheltered public space and promenade – the inhabited roof of Le Corbusier. In addition, the whole building form is attractive and unified when seen from above.

1 Road A
2 Highway B-15
3 Roof Canopy
4 Roof Terrace
5 Road E-1
6 Central Courtyard

View Across Road A

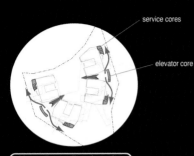

service cores

elevator core

Naturally ventilated service
cores with views out

Continuous vegetation to
landscape terrain beyond

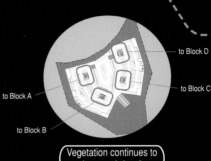

to Block D

to Block C

to Block A

to Block B

Vegetation continues to
lower sub-level

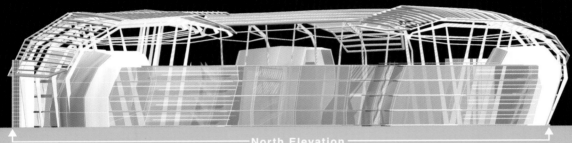

North Elevation

Coupled with the landscaped roof is the inclusion of landscaped bridges which enable the planting and
species to extend continuously both across the site from the central gardens outwards, and upwards on

Sequential Views Driving Along Highway B-15

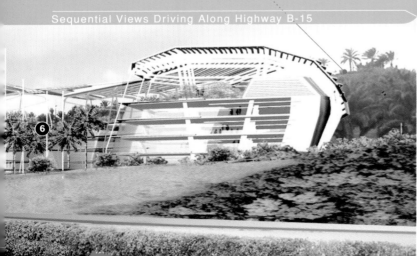

6

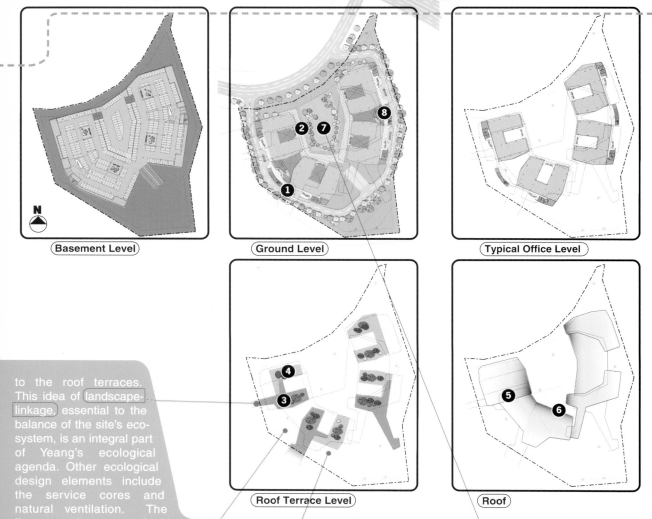

Basement Level

Ground Level

Typical Office Level

Roof Terrace Level

Roof

N

to the roof terraces. This idea of landscape-linkage, essential to the balance of the site's eco-system, is an integral part of Yeang's ecological agenda. Other ecological design elements include the service cores and natural ventilation. The linear service cores shield the entire length of the eastern and western facades on the periphery of the plan. In common with Yeang's skyscraper series, these cores are naturally ventilated and incorporate openings to introduce natural light and reduce energy consumption, while also providing views outwards for orientation and connectivity with the surrounding environment. In being positioned out-board of the plan the linear cores are literally and collectively a massive solar shield. At the same, the office floor-plates are left free as open columnar spaces. The basement car parking is naturally ventilated and is inflected by the landscaped central Court. The courtyard is at the centre of the life of the building, including a canopied out door leisure terrace, and air-flow across the courtyard is encouraged by the open spaces between the office forms. The overall plan is deceptively simple, at first sight, but it is ingeniously assembled, and unified by the three elements of overarching hover-roof canopy, sweeping landscape bridges and the courtyard with its shared external Promenade, on the inner edge. Converse to Yeang's high-rise ecological

9 aluminum louvered panels
10 structure + multi-layered stringers
11 elevator + access cores
12 service cores
13 roof terrace
14 office floor plates

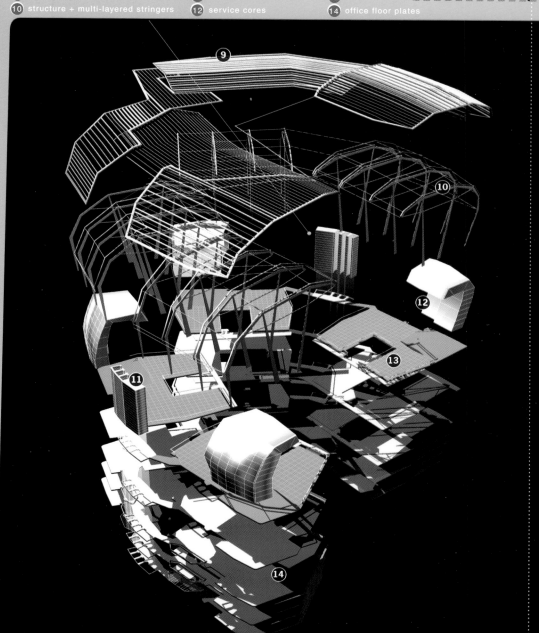

Ground Voids
Shared Promenade
Vegetation Bridges
Roof Garden
Canopy Roof
Metal Mesh Membrane
Protected Courtyard
Perimeter Driveway

**> >> Er Mei Subscraper is served by air-wells or atria, t
air-wells have enclosable skylights to ventilate the low**

architecture of vertical urbanism and landscape, Enterprise 4 is the ecological architecture of the ground-plane –

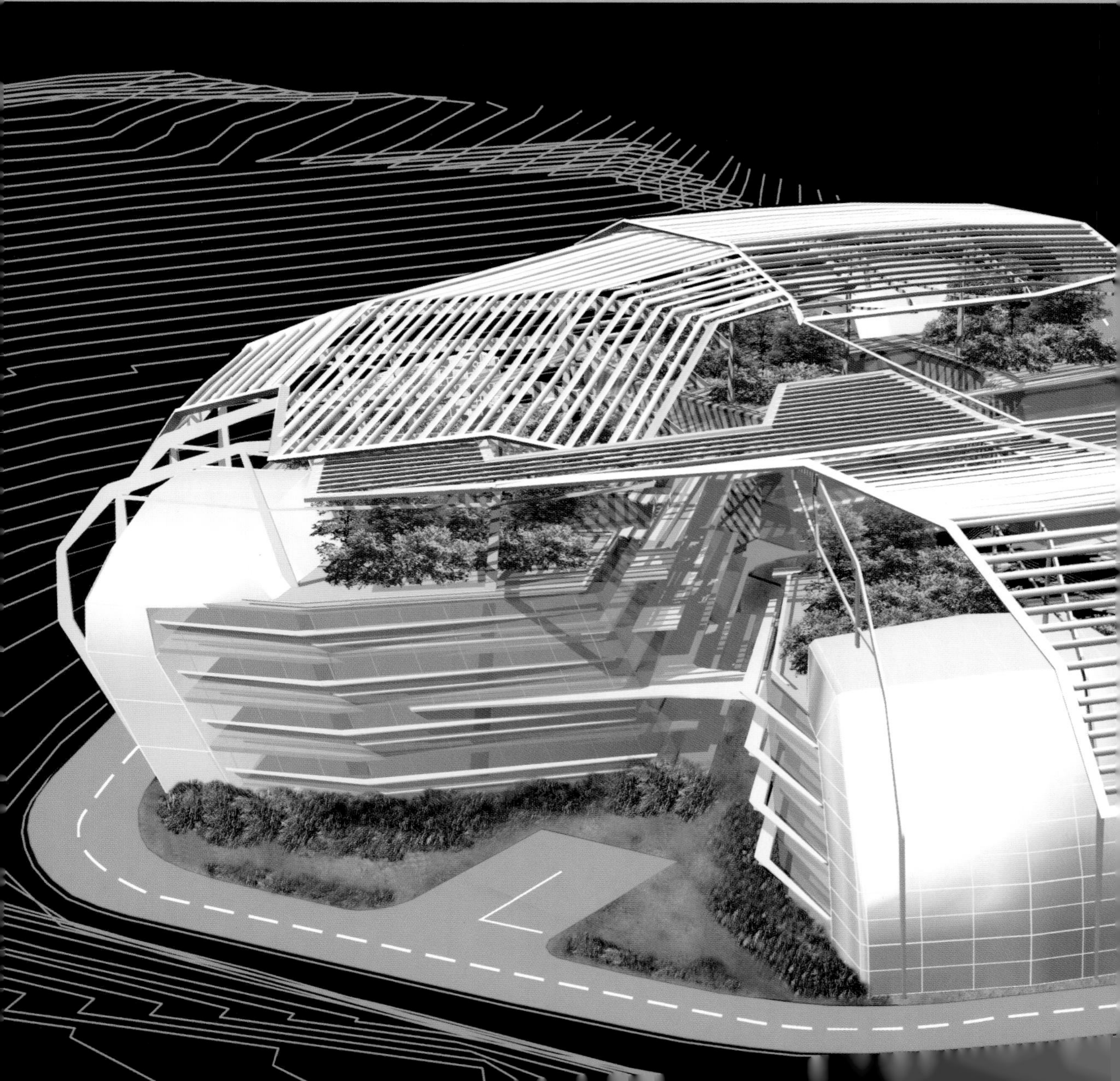

ring light and ventilation into the sunken spaces. The
r levels in summer and to contain heat-in ...   >   >>

0 2 3

a form of built landscape. But it is related to the eco-towers as a distinctive example of the sunpath type.

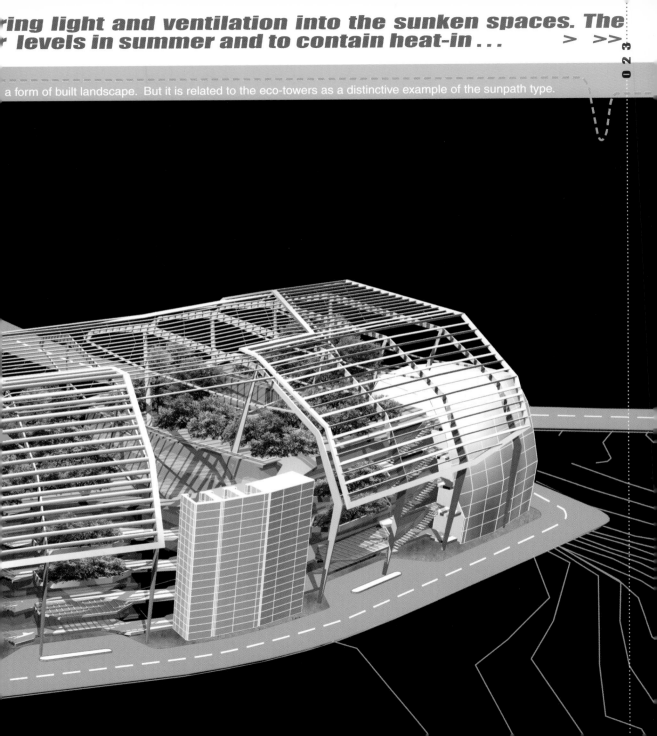

> >> during winter. This is a prototypical bioclimatic

2.1 2.2 2.3 2.4 2.5 2.6 2.7 2.8 2.9 2.10 2.11 2.12 2.

content page 1.1 1.2 1.3

tech-linx

built-up area: 29 285 sq.m plantation area: 16 101

technology park

rks]:50.087sq.m nett:21 799 sq.m Areas Tech-Linx Sdn. Bhd.Client 101.40°E Longitude 2.45°N Latitude Cyberjaya,MalaysiaLocation ▬ **Project Data** ▬

B

A————A

B

Key plan

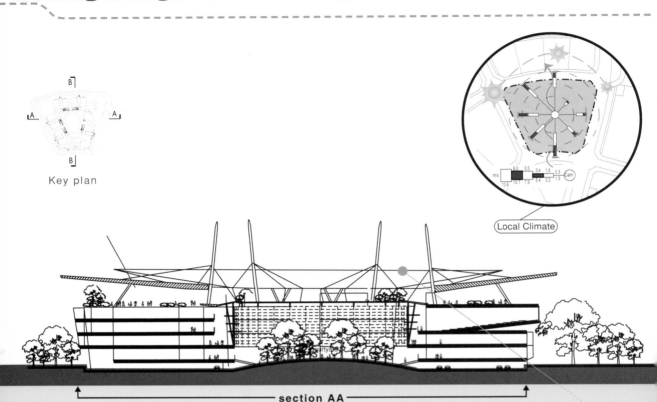

Local Climate

— section AA —

The Tech-Linx project appears to related to Enterprise 4 in its typology - that of a central Courtyard form, with encircling units of space covered and protected by massive hovering roof canopies with independent structure as an umbrella-roof applied to a campus-like arrangement. This is a flagship project for a corporate headquarters for software business. The site is in Cyberjaya, Malaysia, and is a heavily landscaped proposition. In response to the brief for an environmentally responsive and energy efficient building, with intelligent systems, to provide a user-friendly environment for tenants in the IT industry, Yeang has delivered a comprehensive project.

ntain a range of major bioclimatic and ecological con-
ve systems integral to each design. The two . . .   >   > >

0 2 7

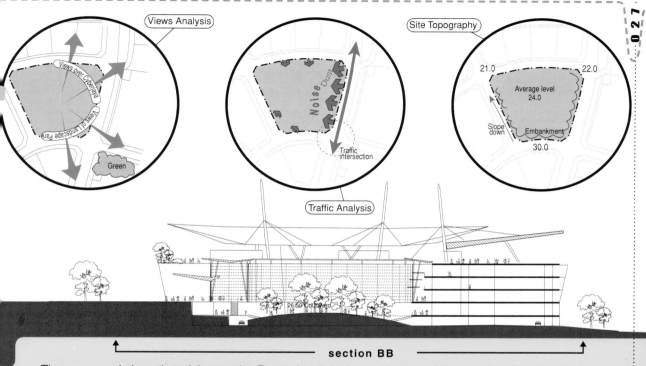

Views Analysis

Views over Cyberjaya

Views of Landscape Park

Green

Site Topography

21.0   22.0

Average level
24.0

Slope
down   Embankment

30.0

Noise Dust

Traffic
intersection

Traffic Analysis

26.50 Courtyard

section BB

There are variations that elaborate the Enterprise 4 design, and extend his principles. The plan-form incorporates two sets of linked open-floor offices, suitable for multiple tenancy, together with two further buildings with communal and conference facilities. The whole 'V' form Courtyard complex is interlinked by a promenade, enclosing a naturally-ventilated space with dense forest vegetation; a further floating canopy defines the main entrance and forms a covered porte-cochère. The buildings are raised above sunken parking, that all are naturally lit and ventilated. The whole form is surrounded and infilled with extensive planting, including the open roof terraces shaded by oversailing fabric roof-canopies. The peripheral site areas also in-

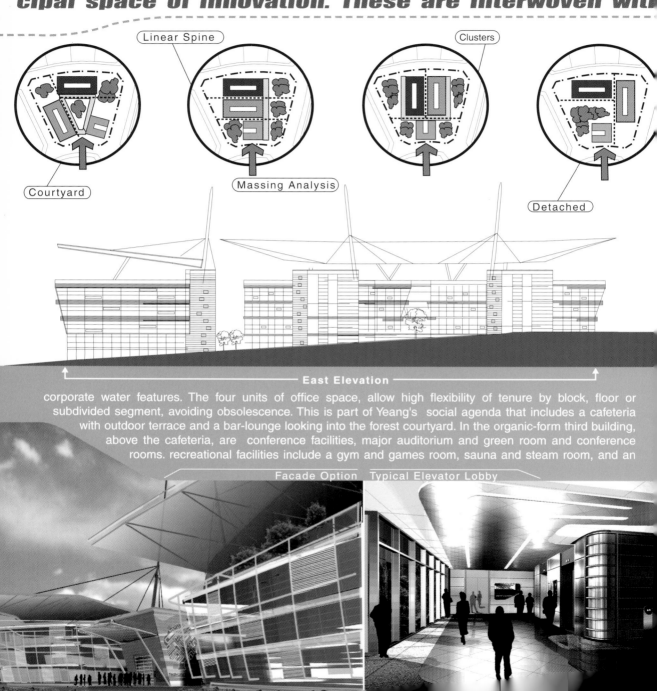

> > > **crucial conditions of these designs are the foot cipal space of innovation. These are interwoven wit**

Linear Spine

Courtyard

Massing Analysis

Clusters

Detached

East Elevation

corporate water features. The four units of office space, allow high flexibility of tenure by block, floor or subdivided segment, avoiding obsolescence. This is part of Yeang's social agenda that includes a cafeteria with outdoor terrace and a bar-lounge looking into the forest courtyard. In the organic-form third building, above the cafeteria, are conference facilities, major auditorium and green room and conference rooms. recreational facilities include a gym and games room, sauna and steam room, and an

Facade Option   Typical Elevator Lobby

rint the spreading plan form, and the section the prin-
e landform-landscape. Yeang's ecological . . .   > >>

029

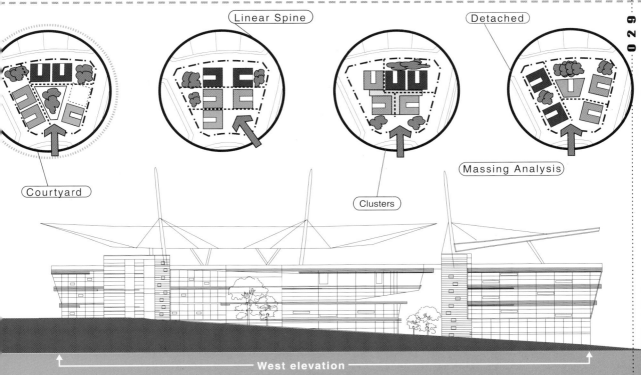

Courtyard

Linear Spine

Clusters

Detached

Massing Analysis

West elevation

extensive crèche provides staff with work-access flexibility. The sociability of this provision, together with the extensive planted roof terraces and sheltered public space provides both a social hub and areas for out-of-hours relaxation and informal meetings. Central to the social program is the visual relationship of the user to the external natural environment from within. This is achieved by a maximum glass-to-glass width of an office space of 16m, which delivers a naturally lit space and cross ventilation potential.

Model View Of Internal Garden

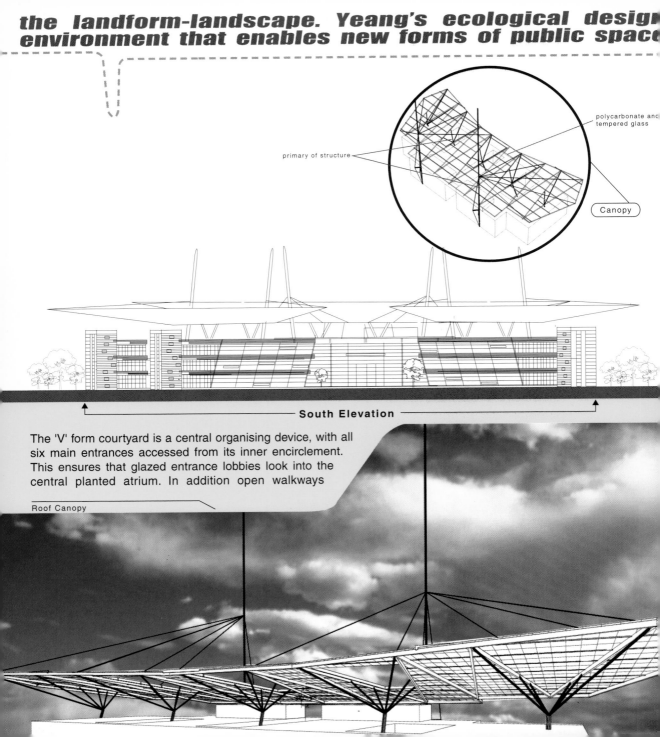

polycarbonate and
tempered glass

primary of structure

Canopy

— **South Elevation** —

Roof Canopy

The 'V' form courtyard is a central organising device, with all
six main entrances accessed from its inner encirclement.
This ensures that glazed entrance lobbies look into the
central planted atrium. In addition open walkways

Canopy Openning
over courtyard

Polycarbonate or
glass tempered

Polycarbonate &
suframe

Cross
Beams

secondary roof
structure

Steel Truss

Column

(Structure Diagram)

(Basement Level 1)

(Basement Level 2)

connecting the office units and shade balconies on the external facades, ensure an atmosphere of openness and spatial release, that is unexpected on an urban site. Taken overall, this assemblage of precise machine-made forms, with the tensile fabric roof which shades and weather protects the roof-terraces, provides an architecture of transparency and calm - a series of garden tent-pavilions that are juxtaposed with extensive, linked, luxuriant water features and forest planting. Seen from above, it is as though three great white butterflies have settled on the existing glass pavilions, set in their forest domain. This organic analogy is perhaps not altogether inappropriate, as Yeang frequently makes reference to natural organisms in his own books and lectures. Yeang's system of ecological design, based on interconnectedness of all criteria and evaluations within the design process, is explored here in a series of appraisals. These include External and Internal Dependencies, and a series of Passive Low Energy Responses. The external considerations are

Auditorium

Washroom

>>> to his architecture. These formative qualities en into an innovative architectural form, based on the appl

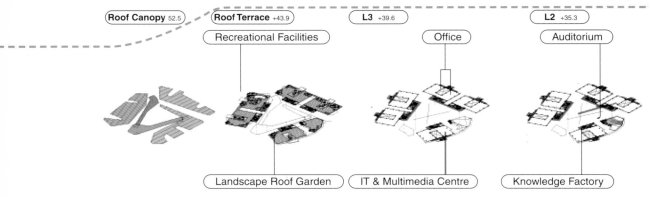

Roof Canopy 52.5

Roof Terrace +43.9

L3 +39.6

L2 +35.3

Recreational Facilities

Office

Auditorium

Landscape Roof Garden

IT & Multimedia Centre

Knowledge Factory

considerations are the site's ecosystem and its properties. Yeang concludes that the site is not virgin territory and has had much of its original topsoil, flora and fauna removed. His strategy is at once to rebuild the biodiversity of the site as a man-made ecosystem. In practice this includes a densely planted edge to the site, using indigenous forest species, which in turn form a natural buffer to the surrounding road traffic and noise. This policy is continued into the central courtyard and up onto the shaded roof terraces, beneath the fabric canopies, ensuring continuity of landscape. As with Enterprise 4, it is an architecture of built landscape and minimalist pavilions. Water is a further external consideration, both in pond configurations surrounding the site and in terms of collection and recycling. Surface water is percolated back into the ground at the car-park level, and internal courts with planting are introduced at this basement position to ensure maximum natural ventilation and lighting. Notably, roof rainwater is recycled as a grey-water reticulation system. Specifically, rainwater run-off from the roof canopies is to be used for toilet flushing, washing and landscape irrigation. The Internal Dependencies are then explored in parallel, and relate to the building's environmental operational systems under four levels of provision: *Passive mode: low energy/without electro mechanical *Mixed mode: partial electro mechanical and ambient energy *Full mode: active systems/low energy *Productive mode: on site generation/Photovoltaic system or other*

Yeang's strategy is to maximise the usage of passive-mode systems to minimise energy consumption. The remaining energy needs are met by the other three modes. In addition the Cyberjaya chilled water network has been utilised, on the basis that district cooling systems reduce consumption by meeting all the site's cooling requirements, en masse. Finally the Passive Low Energy Responses in relation to the tropical climate, include Sun-shading, Water Features, Building Colour Configuration and Orientation, and Landscaping. Sun-shading dominates the overall design-form with the three butterfly-umbrellas over the pavilions, which reduce the buildings' reception of solar impact and consequently their air-conditioning load. Water features, peripheral to the buildings, contribute to the lowering of ambient temperatures. Building Colour is generally light (shades of white), and therefore non-heat absorbing on the exterior. Building configuration is central to the low-energy concept. A perimeter Courtyard form, with open landscaped core, is formed by three major volumes with weather protected inter-link walkways. This open, encircled configuration promotes cross-ventilation and natural light throughout the loosely arranged complex. Building orientation is resolved by office sun-shading and the huge butterfly fabric-canopies. Internal courts provide cross-ventilation in all office spaces with openable windows on all glazed facades. At the same time, the maximum width of 16 metres ensures day lighting, without direct sunlight penetration into the interior space. Landscaping is a major factor: applied to the internal courts, central atrium and roof terraces, the vegetation insulates the building by reducing thermal impact. Especially applicable to the extensive roof terraces, the planters and gardens provide thermal protection and oxygenation, and eliminate the need for man-made

le Yeang to transform a relatively conventional brief ation of ecological principles. His buildings ... **> >>**

033

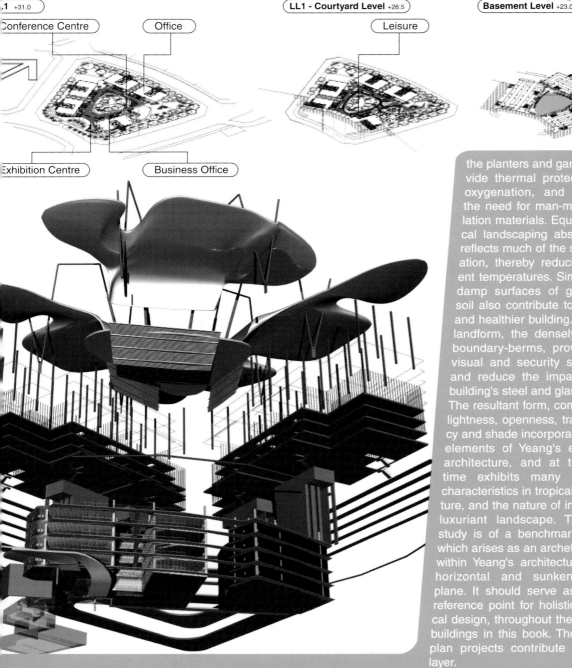

.1 +31.0

Conference Centre | Office

LL1 - Courtyard Level +26.5 | Leisure

Basement Level +23.0

Exhibition Centre | Business Office

the planters and gardens provide thermal protection and oxygenation, and eliminate the need for man-made insulation materials. Equally, vertical landscaping absorbs and reflects much of the solar radiation, thereby reducing ambient temperatures. Similarly the damp surfaces of grass and soil also contribute to a cooler and healthier building. A further landform, the densely planted boundary-berms, provide both visual and security screening, and reduce the impact of the building's steel and glass nature. The resultant form, composed of lightness, openness, transparency and shade incorporates all the elements of Yeang's ecological architecture, and at the same time exhibits many time-held characteristics in tropical architecture, and the nature of inhabitated luxuriant landscape. This case study is of a benchmark project, which arises as an archetypal form within Yeang's architecture of the horizontal and sunken ground plane. It should serve as a basic reference point for holistic ecological design, throughout the series of buildings in this book. The masterplan projects contribute a further layer.

university of
malaysia

al'quran

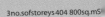

3no.sofstoreys 404 800sq.mS

nottingham,
masterplan

'rehal'

430sq.m gross:70 820sq.m Areas nottingham universityclient 101.40 E Longitude 2.57 N Latitude Semenyih, Selangor Location — **Project Data** —

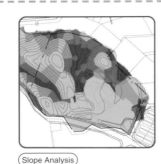

Slope Analysis

Natural Drainage

Land Suitability for Development

Key plan

A   A

Student Residence   Central Administration

Section AA

The masterplan and its overall form is based on two major principles, which determine the footprint. The 'cradle of learning' as an idea, drawn from the Rehal book cradle traditionally holding the al-Quran open, is translated into a three dimensional arrangement of central hub and two major covered promenades linking ranges of attached buildings. This architectural arrangement is then interlaced with continuous planting - a strategy of green-fingers - which is the underlying theme of the whole project. Yeang's overall proposition is therefore infused with Malay references, and yet related to the Nottingham UK. campus, in the use of water and lush landscaping. In his analysis of the site, Yeang has

1 Central Administration
2 Main Chancellor
3 Residential
4 Academic Block
5 Central Teaching Centre
6 Central Catering

Masterplan

N

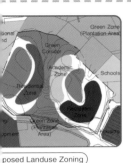

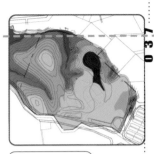

posed Landuse Zoning

Public and Private Realm

Solar Path and Wind Direction

Topography Diagram

Central Learning Centre / Academic Block

assessed all aspects of its condition from Slope and Drainage analysis through to Solar Path and Wind Direction. The site is accessed by one major (Entrance Forecourt) with guard house, which controls all traffic both vehicular and pedestrian, including public transport. Public Entrance leads off the Forecourt, by-passing the guard house, and encouraging visitors, commuting students and the surrounding community to make use of the facilities. Alongside the main entrance is a major artificial lake to the north, and a 500 place student car park and sport centre to the south. At the crux of the project is the Central Administration and Senate Chamber, marking the

Model Aerial View
View of Student Residence Blocks

'rehal'

Level 01

N

Central Learning Centre   Central Administration

major point of arrival and the joining of the two extensive, sweeping linear spines of academic buildings arcing to the east, and the Student Residences and Catering to the west. As a major entrance statement, the design incorporates a botanical atrium, and associated with the Senate Hall is a covered Event Plaza with a lightweight 'Facade Tower' which acts as a wind exhaust to the public space. This wind scoop and air funnel tower is used to induce air movement from the valley, and has an integral extract fan to mechanically assist air movement when wind levels are low. The design takes advantage of the natural landform to enhance air movement and provide cooling for the promenade areas. The major configurations of buildings also act as wind walls that channel air towards the wind-tower. The wind-tower and its lightweight membrane roof is thus the major emblematic form of the university campus, together with the covered

Night View

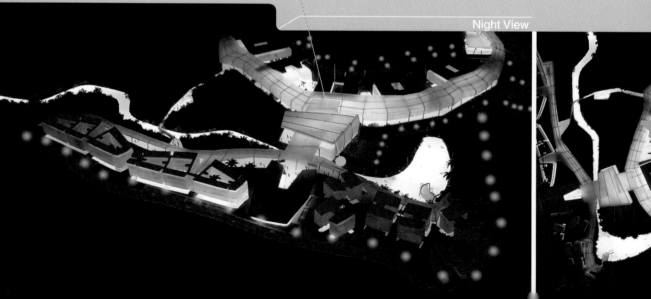

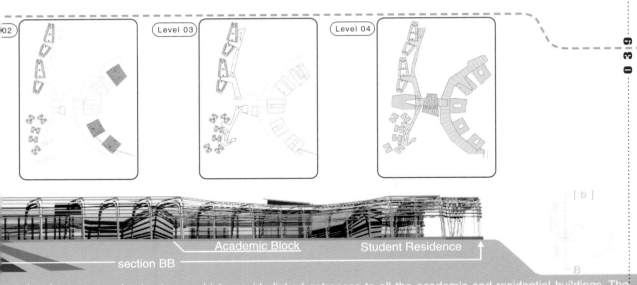

02   Level 03   Level 04

Academic Block   Student Residence

section BB

[b]

B

pedestrian promenade structures, which provide linked entrances to all the academic and residential buildings. The promenade structures take a similar form to the wind-tower, that of a repeating portal-frame, reminiscent of Aalto, and covered in a continuous light membrane.   These great promenades of public space, which are exclusively pedestrian, enable users to walk the whole campus in a pleasant, shaded, outdoor boulevard environment.   The vehicular traffic is entirely separated to ensure a safer network for pedestrian users. Seen at night, the illuminated covered outdoor spaces of the Event Plaza, Wind-tower and Pedestrian Promenades completely define the overall design threaded into its luxuriant landscape of reforestation, vegetation and water courses.

Entrance Forecourt   Canopy over Promenade

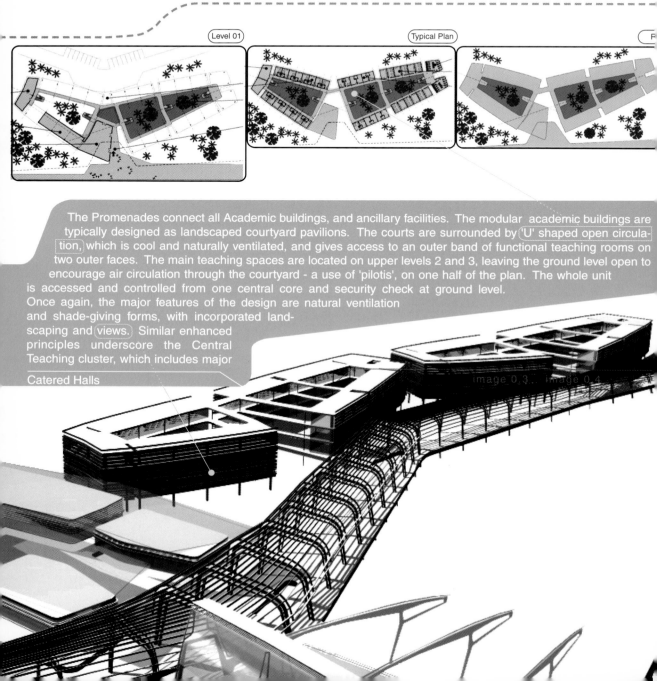

Level 01

Typical Plan

The Promenades connect all Academic buildings, and ancillary facilities. The modular academic buildings are typically designed as landscaped courtyard pavilions. The courts are surrounded by 'U' shaped open circulation, which is cool and naturally ventilated, and gives access to an outer band of functional teaching rooms on two outer faces. The main teaching spaces are located on upper levels 2 and 3, leaving the ground level open to encourage air circulation through the courtyard - a use of 'pilotis', on one half of the plan. The whole unit is accessed and controlled from one central core and security check at ground level.

Once again, the major features of the design are natural ventilation and shade-giving forms, with incorporated landscaping and views. Similar enhanced principles underscore the Central Teaching cluster, which includes major

Catered Halls

Level 01 | Typical Plan | Roof

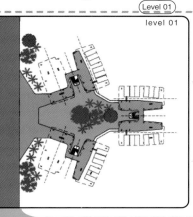

level 01

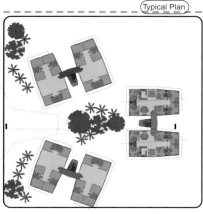

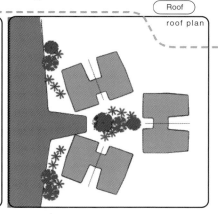

roof plan

cludes major Lecture Theatres and seminar rooms. The Residential Accommodation is divided into three main complexes - two clusters of self-catered, six bed flats and two sets of catered units. These complexes are located on the median lines of the contours to reduce earthworks, and are attached to the main circulation promenade. The whole forms an Environmentally Sustainable Campus, whose basic underlying masterplan strategy is a response to the natural forces of the site. (Buildings) feature devices for sun shading, cross-ventilation, and rain-water collection.

Self-Catered Halls

> \> \>> **informal outdoor meetings and other events, lei**
these typological themes of courtyard and canopy. The

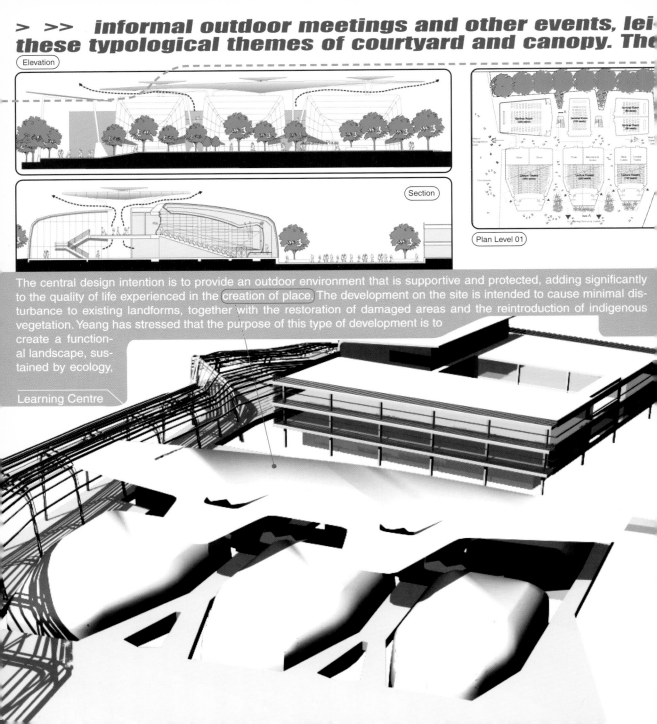

Elevation

Section

Plan Level 01

The central design intention is to provide an outdoor environment that is supportive and protected, adding significantly to the quality of life experienced in the creation of place. The development on the site is intended to cause minimal disturbance to existing landforms, together with the restoration of damaged areas and the reintroduction of indigenous vegetation. Yeang has stressed that the purpose of this type of development is to create a functional landscape, sustained by ecology,

Learning Centre

ure and recreation. There are endless variations of
Malaysian Design Technology Centre includes . . .   > >>

043

> >> a central courtyard plaza, but this is covered by

um within the roof structure itself. The massive mush

Centralised Planting

Dispersed Planting

Continuous Planting
[Green-Fingers]

The above three diagrams illustrate alternative
ways to integrate vegetation and landscape into
the city. The third pattern is adopted here.

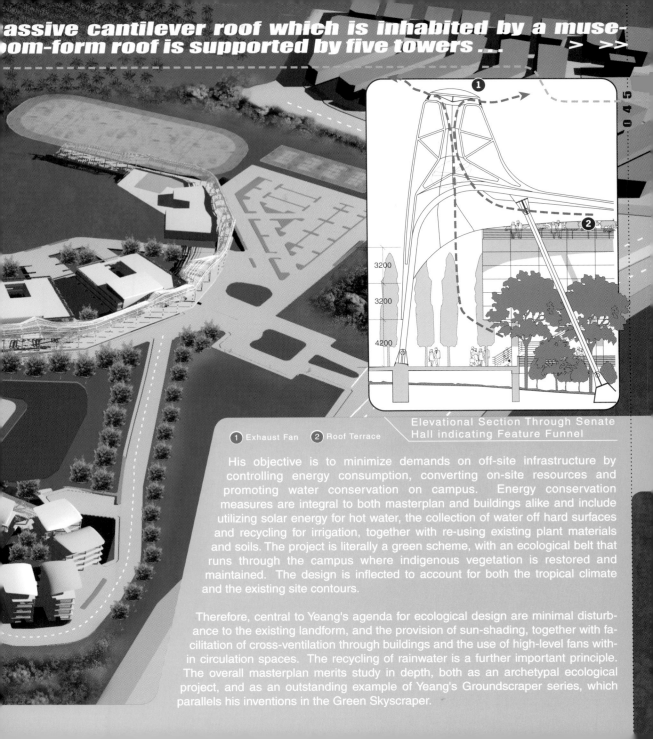

① Exhaust Fan ② Roof Terrace

Elevational Section Through Senate Hall indicating Feature Funnel

His objective is to minimize demands on off-site infrastructure by controlling energy consumption, converting on-site resources and promoting water conservation on campus. Energy conservation measures are integral to both masterplan and buildings alike and include utilizing solar energy for hot water, the collection of water off hard surfaces and recycling for irrigation, together with re-using existing plant materials and soils. The project is literally a green scheme, with an ecological belt that runs through the campus where indigenous vegetation is restored and maintained. The design is inflected to account for both the tropical climate and the existing site contours.

Therefore, central to Yeang's agenda for ecological design are minimal disturbance to the existing landform, and the provision of sun-shading, together with facilitation of cross-ventilation through buildings and the use of high-level fans within circulation spaces. The recycling of rainwater is a further important principle. The overall masterplan merits study in depth, both as an archetypal ecological project, and as an outstanding example of Yeang's Groundscraper series, which parallels his inventions in the Green Skyscraper.

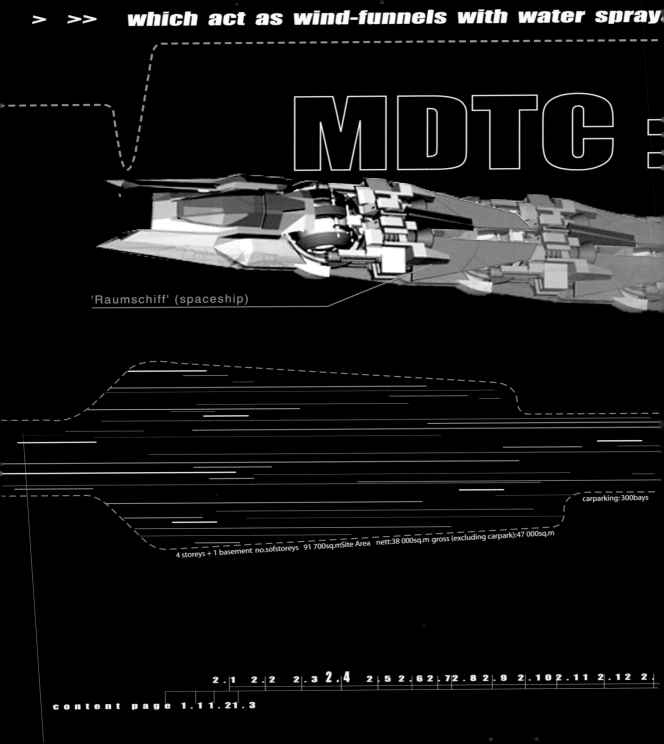

MDTC :

'Raumschiff' (spaceship)

carparking: 300bays

4 storeys + 1 basement no.sofstoreys 91 700sq.mSite Area   nett:38 000sq.m gross (excluding carpark):47 000sq.m

2 . 1   2 . 2   2 . 3 2 . 4   2 . 5 2 . 6 2 . 7 2 . 8 2 . 9   2 . 1 0 2 . 1 1   2 . 1 2   2 .

c o n t e n t   p a g e   1 . 1 1 . 2 1 . 3

malaysia design
technology
centre

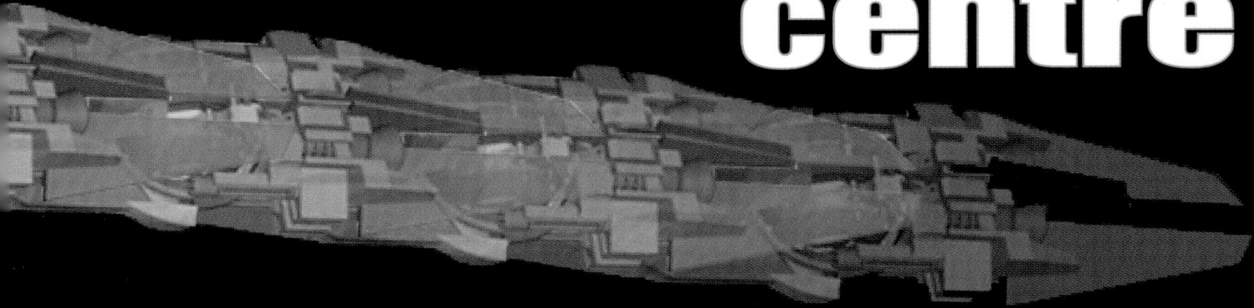

Areas LimKokWing Institute of Creative Technoogy client

101.40°E Longitude 2.57°N Latitude Cyberjaya, Selangor Location ▬ **Project Data** ▬

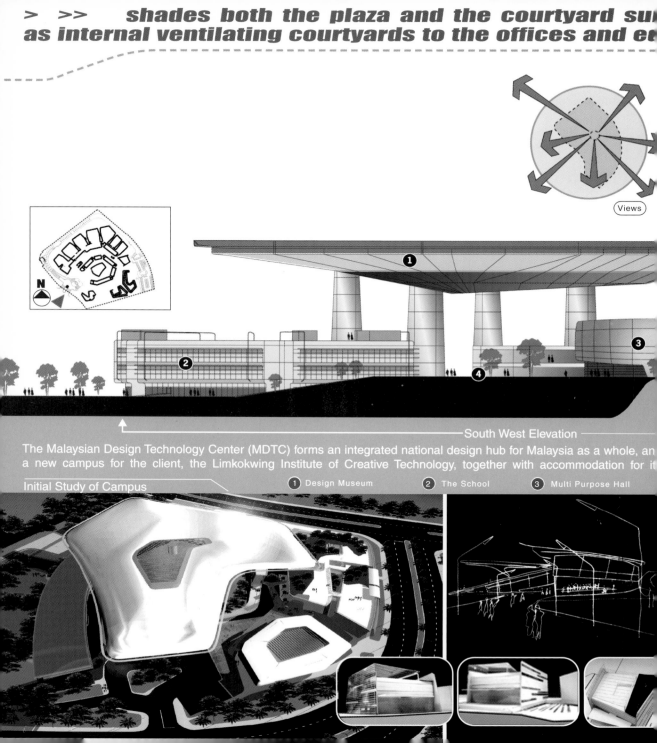

Views

① ② ③ ④

South West Elevation

The Malaysian Design Technology Center (MDTC) forms an integrated national design hub for Malaysia as a whole, an|
a new campus for the client, the Limkokwing Institute of Creative Technology, together with accommodation for it|

Initial Study of Campus

① Design Museum   ② The School   ③ Multi Purpose Hall

und of low-rise forms. In turn these contain Air-Wells
cational spaces. Taichung City Civic Center ... > >>

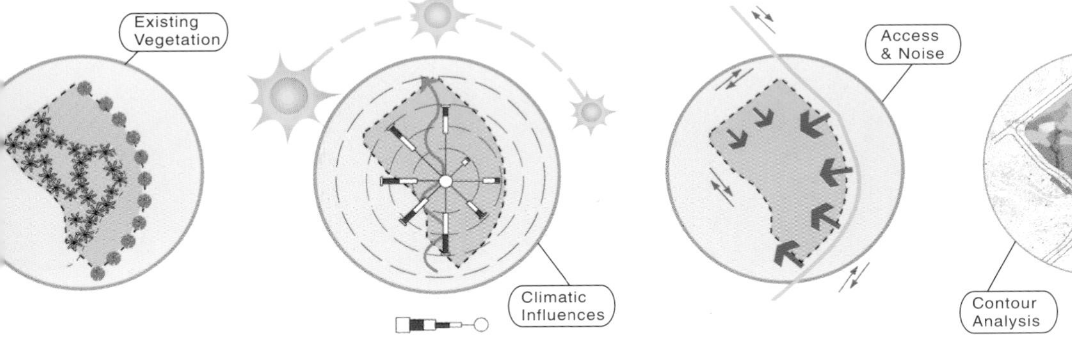

Existing Vegetation
Climatic Influences
Access & Noise
Contour Analysis

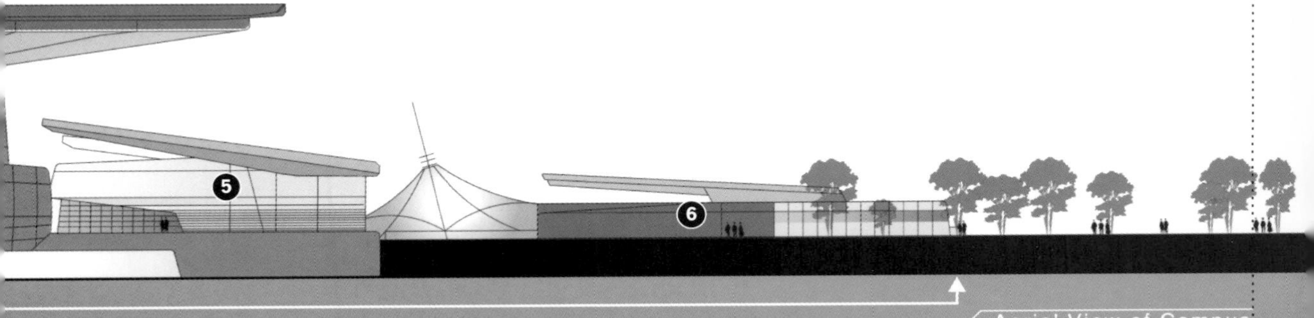

5
6

Aerial View of Campus

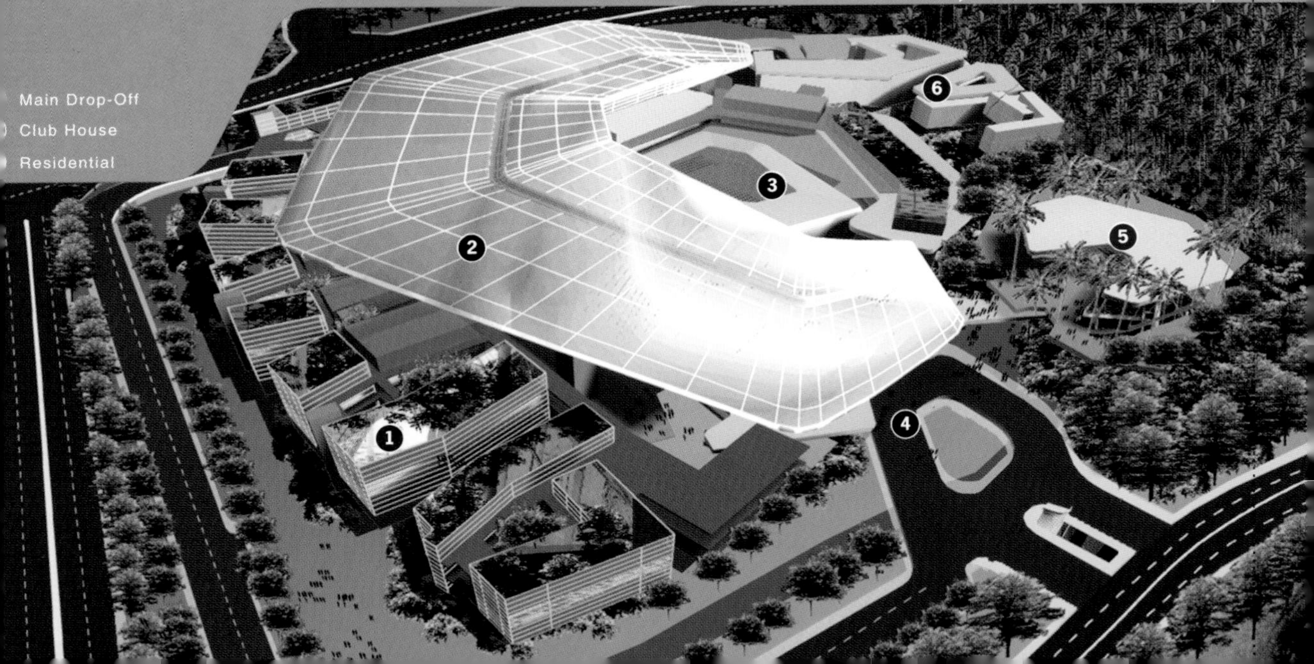

Main Drop-Off
Club House
Residential
1
2
3
4
5
6

(Masterplan)

(Level 1)

(Level 2)

students. The site is again at Cyberjaya, Selangor, on a prime, gateway, hill-top location - so it is in every sense a flagship project. The major programme includes an International Design Museum, exhibition spaces, professional design-office suites and commercial office space, together with the Limkokwing Institute campus accommodation. A basement

Level 3

Level 6

Level Roof

North East Elevation

provides 260 car parking spaces. Yeang's project summarises its mission as being about Innovation, Technology and Multimedia. The functional programme is identified as facilitating events, multimedia activities, incorporated flexibility, and

View of Drop-Off

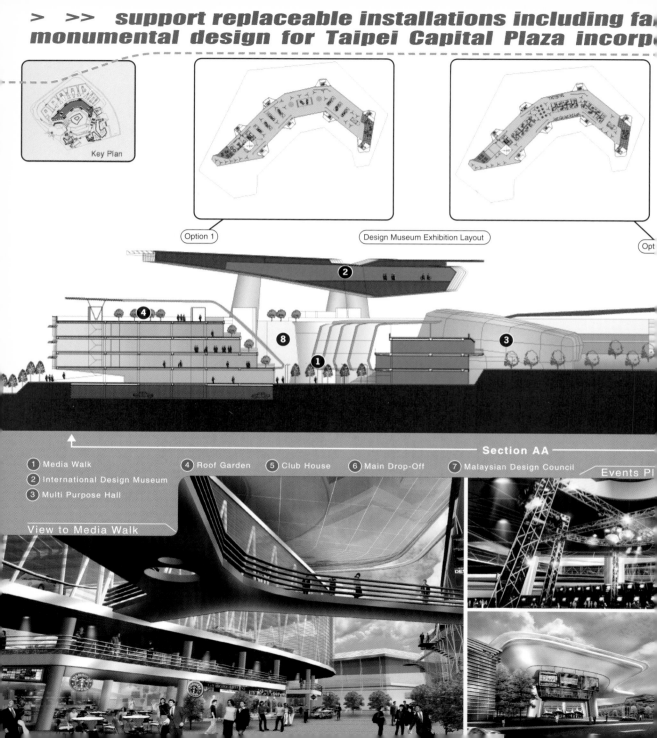

Key Plan

Option 1

Design Museum Exhibition Layout

Opt

Section AA

① Media Walk
② International Design Museum
③ Multi Purpose Hall
④ Roof Garden
⑤ Club House
⑥ Main Drop-Off
⑦ Malaysian Design Council

Events Pl

View to Media Walk

Level 1

Level 2

Level 3

School of Architecture Furniture Layout

Level 1

Level 2

Level 3

N

Outdoor Terraces ⑨ Academic Block

and bio-climatic design. These categories include a wide range of scenarios and features such as graduation, banquet and concert events, a media walk, lectures and films, together with digital displays, multi-function atrium discussion space and flexible partitioning of spaces. The bio-climatic agenda focuses on controlled natural daylighting and ventilation, shade, weather protection and cross-ventilation with integrated landscaping and vegetation - both on

Entrance and Drop-Off

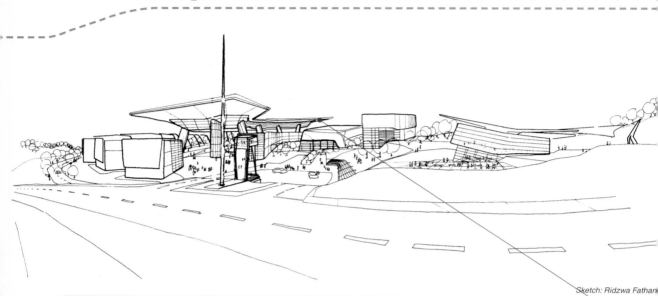

Sketch: Ridzwa Fathan

ground levels and roof terraces. The overall design is once more an organic courtyard form, with a super-cantilever hovering-inhabited roof at its centre, supported on five cores within the court itself. The courtyard therefore forms a sheltered central Events Plaza. The peripheral accommodation includes commercial office space, with solar-shield service cores on the west face, the education institute, a multi-purpose auditorium with special clusters of seating, linked lecture halls with revolving stage, and a major library. The most important formal innovations are the elevated museum and the upward-spiraling Super Gallery for exhibitions, which lines the inner edge of the courtyard, surrounding the Events Plaza. This ramped winding space lifts above the landscaped office roofs below and is both served and shielded by the linear sets of service cores on the west. The ramped Super-Gallery, in turn, is linked to the central, triple height Exhibition space which forms the Design Museum and inhabits the main sectional area of the dish-form balanced cantilever hover-roof. The whole roof structure is supported on five access cores. These cores are structured to form wind-funnels, which coupled with water-spray 'misters' bring comfort-

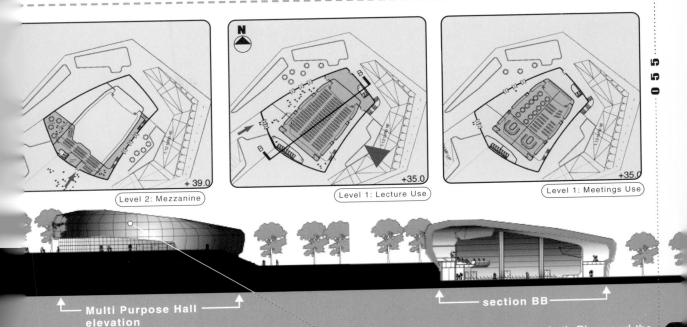

N

Level 2: Mezzanine   + 39.0

Level 1: Lecture Use   +35.0

Level 1: Meetings Use   +35.0

Multi Purpose Hall elevation

section BB

coolth to the Events Plaza. The super-cantilever roof-dish forms an overall shade umbrella to both Plaza and the low-rise peripheral buildings, combining the principles of open-enclosure and weather protection. The streamlined curvilinear roof is the emblematic bio-climatic symbol of the design, and its most dramatic and distinctive formal element. Yeang has determined that the most essential elements of his Groundscraper series are the crucial footprint and the section - in this case the court form and the inhabited roof-structure, both integral to the bio-climatic response.

Further bio-climatic elements include the provision of 'air wells' as internally-ventilating courtyards to the low-rise offices and education institute. These atria also provide natural light in the institute areas. The roofs of the low buildings are all extensively landscaped and form spaces for outdoor events and sports activities. In turn, the landscaping forms another thermal-shield at roof level, in response to the tropical sun-path. The mixed-mode servicing of the project is joined by a grey-water recycling system, as part of the overall ecological agenda.

The MDTC and its loose-circle of permeable buildings is intended to encourage interaction and activities for people working, studying or visiting the complex. With its vibrant mix of design related work and events, commercial studios and youth facilities, the epitome of the MDTC aspiration is immediately visible.

What emerges is the added quality of life, and value, that is a natural product of Yeang's bio-climatic response to the client's design brief. In this case it is vividly evidenced by the hovering-roof which protects the central plaza from sun and rain and is further enhanced by natural cross-ventilation. This major innovative form enables the creation of a major public space, for concerts, exhibitions and other events. While it may be an extension of the brief - a vision beyond the basic programme - it is inextricably part of Yeang's ecological design method, which underscores his new, developing architecture.

DESIGN

Perspective Media Walk

...which incorporate the layered Roof-Canopy . . .

> >>

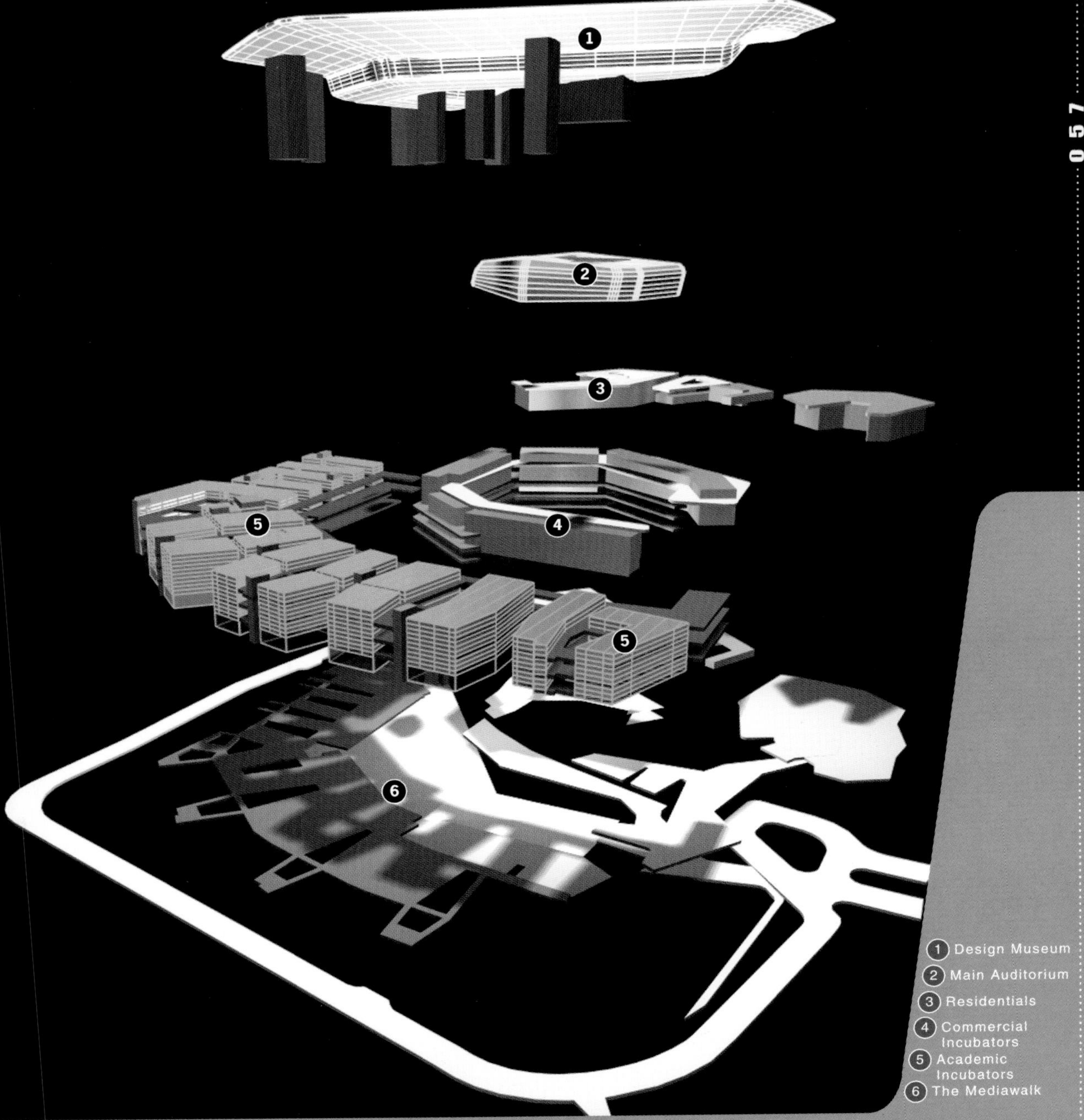
1
2
3
4
5
5
6
1 Design Museum
2 Main Auditorium
3 Residentials
4 Commercial Incubators
5 Academic Incubators
6 The Mediawalk

Exploded Perspective

port mewah

'Silinder Hidraulik' (Hydraulic Cylin

4Storeys (overall height 34m)no.sofstoreys April 2002 Expected Completion date nett: 16 379sq.m. gross: 19 258sq.m. Areas Mewah-Oils Sdn. Bhd.

101.40°E Longitude 2.45°N Latitude Pulau Indah Industrial Park, Port Klang (West Port), Selangor, Malaysia Location —**Project Data** —

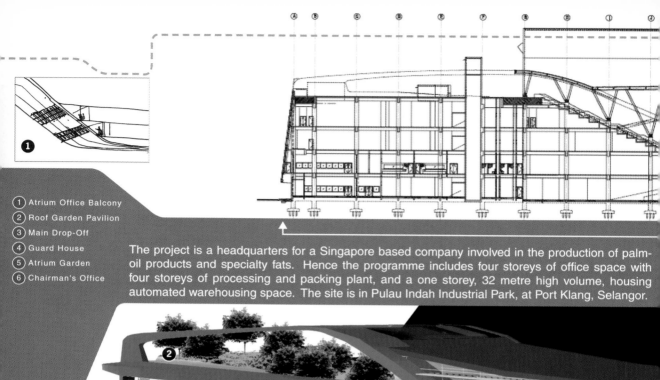

1. Atrium Office Balcony
2. Roof Garden Pavilion
3. Main Drop-Off
4. Guard House
5. Atrium Garden
6. Chairman's Office

The project is a headquarters for a Singapore based company involved in the production of palm-oil products and specialty fats. Hence the programme includes four storeys of office space with four storeys of processing and packing plant, and a one storey, 32 metre high volume, housing automated warehousing space. The site is in Pulau Indah Industrial Park, at Port Klang, Selangor.

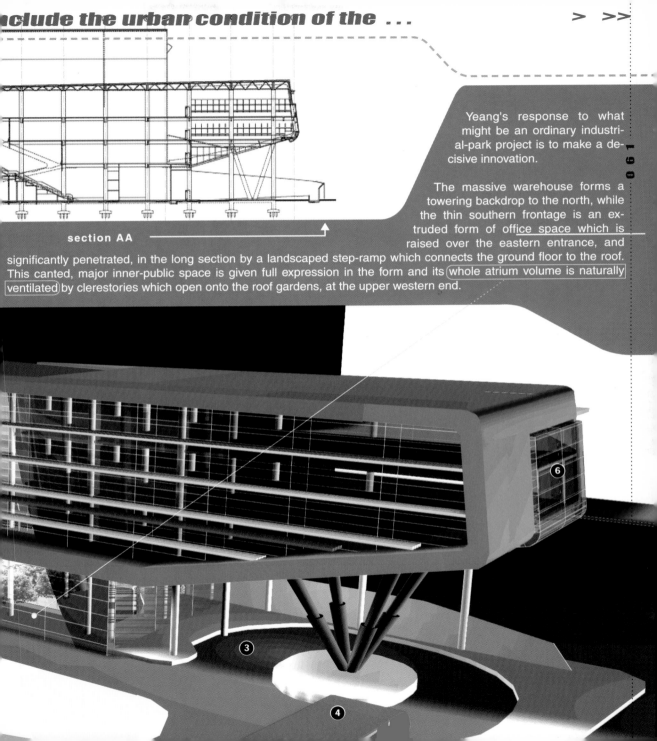

section AA

Yeang's response to what might be an ordinary industrial-park project is to make a decisive innovation.

The massive warehouse forms a towering backdrop to the north, while the thin southern frontage is an extruded form of office space which is raised over the eastern entrance, and significantly penetrated, in the long section by a landscaped step-ramp which connects the ground floor to the roof. This canted, major inner-public space is given full expression in the form and its whole atrium volume is naturally ventilated by clerestories which open onto the roof gardens, at the upper western end.

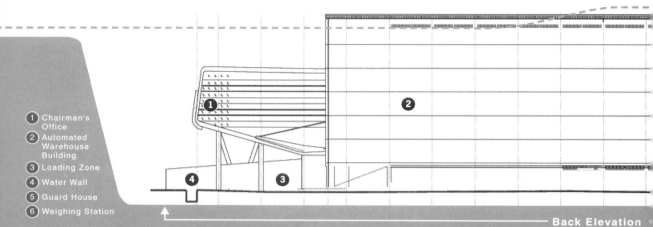

1. Chairman's Office
2. Automated Warehouse Building
3. Loading Zone
4. Water Wall
5. Guard House
6. Weighing Station

— **Back Elevation**

The landscaped ramp-hall is lined by a linear , cascading watercourse and a monumental linear staircase, together with terraces and cafeteria. An outer line of staircases and circulation provides connectivity to the office spaces that are severed by the low-diagonal of the Ramp-Hall and its rising volume.

The landscape of the ramp includes a variety of tropical planting, and the cascading water alongside introduces

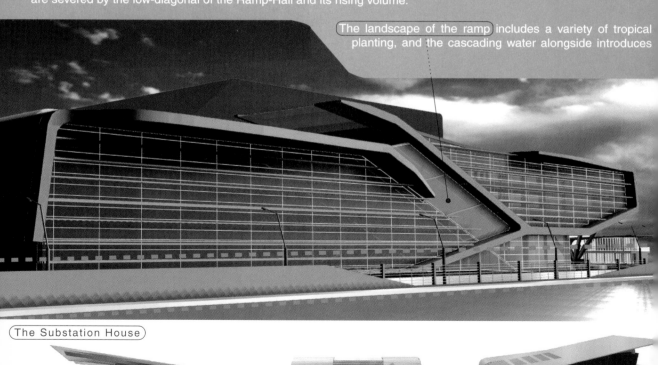

The Substation House

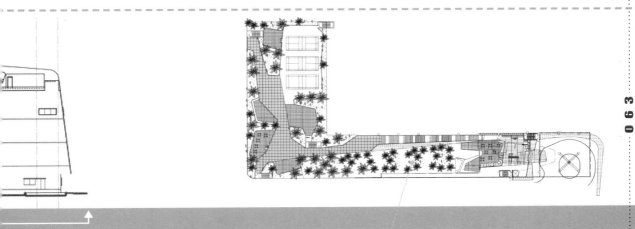

the soothing sound of water, coolth and a sensation of comfort and relaxation for all of the users and visitors.

Yeang has described the continuous landscaped ramp-Hall as an ecological green lung which provides the building with extra quality to both the offices and public space. The sloping atrium space is both passive in its natural ventilation low energy mode, but is designed to switch to a mixed-mode system, if required by internal temperatures. At the same time, the water-cascade acts as a cooling agent for the unenclosed spaces, through passive evaporation.

Entrance View

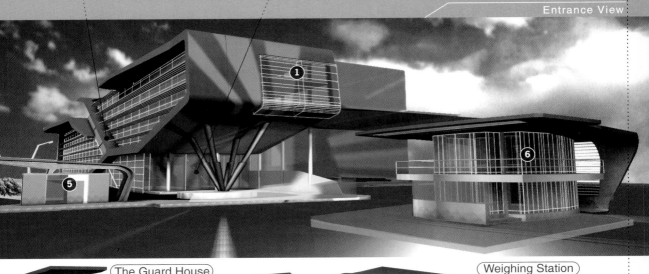

The Guard House

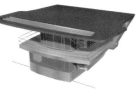

Weighing Station

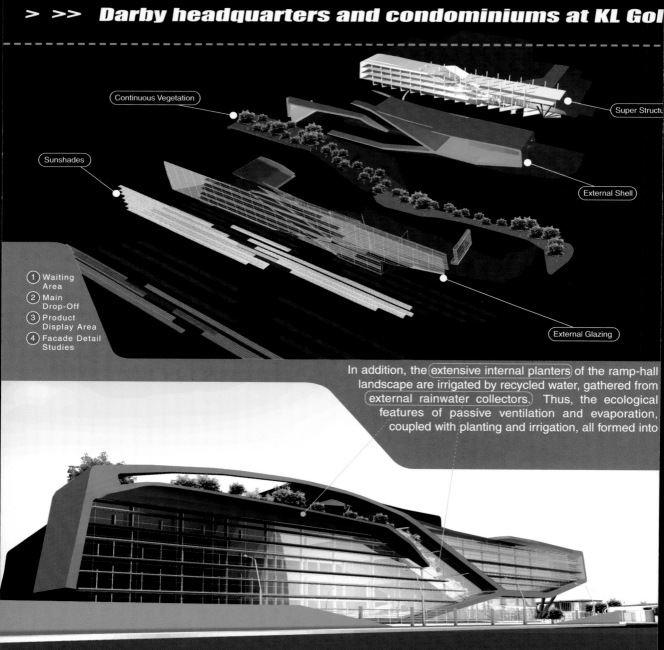

Continuous Vegetation

Super Structu

Sunshades

External Shell

1 Waiting Area
2 Main Drop-Off
3 Product Display Area
4 Facade Detail Studies

External Glazing

In addition, the (extensive internal planters) of the ramp-hall landscape are irrigated by recycled water, gathered from (external rainwater collectors.) Thus, the ecological features of passive ventilation and evaporation, coupled with planting and irrigation, all formed into

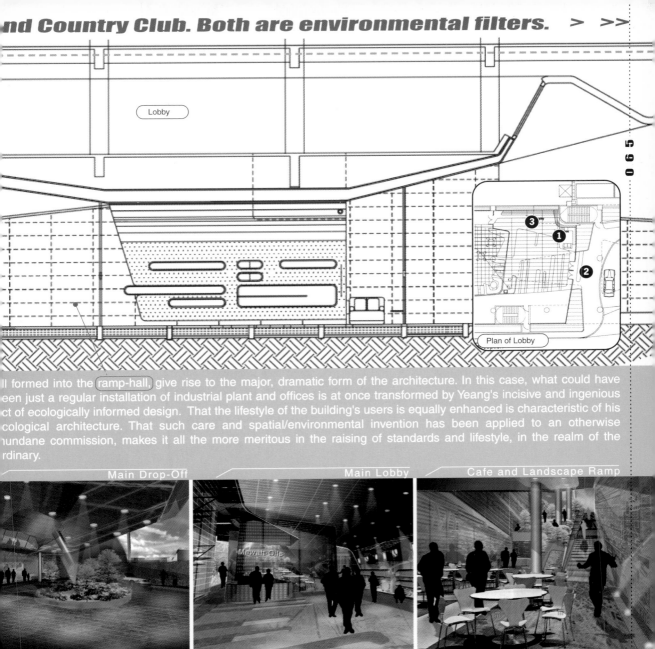

Lobby

Plan of Lobby

ll formed into the ramp-hall, give rise to the major, dramatic form of the architecture. In this case, what could have
een just a regular installation of industrial plant and offices is at once transformed by Yeang's incisive and ingenious
ct of ecologically informed design. That the lifestyle of the building's users is equally enhanced is characteristic of his
cological architecture. That such care and spatial/environmental invention has been applied to an otherwise
undane commission, makes it all the more meritous in the raising of standards and lifestyle, in the realm of the
rdinary.

Main Drop-Off   Main Lobby   Cafe and Landscape Ramp

Mewah Oils

> >> **The latter is a series of trellises and canopie**

2.1 2.2 2.3 2.4 2.5 2.6 2.7 2.8 2.9 2.10 2.11 2.12 2.

content page 1.1 1.2 1.3

BB park

'Movement' Discotheque

Federal Hotel

BB Park

Low Yat Plaza

Capitol Hotel

Sungei Wang Complex

Lot 10 (Shopping Mall)

August 2001 Date of completion 2storeys no.sofstoreys 2 608sq.m. Sit

canopy
kuala lumpur

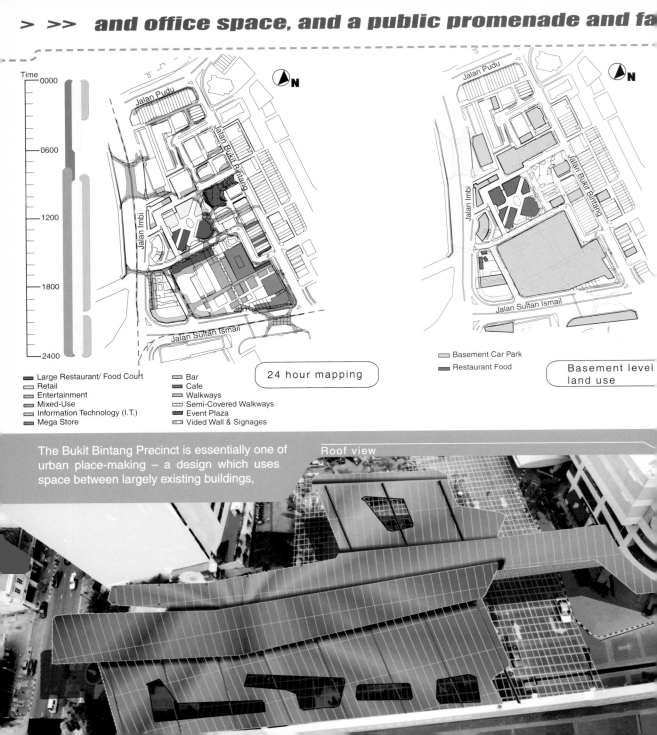

Time

0000
0600
1200
1800
2400

N

Jalan Pudu
Jalan Bukit Bintang
Jalan Imbi
Jalan Sultan Ismail

24 hour mapping

Large Restaurant/ Food Court
Retail
Entertainment
Mixed-Use
Information Technology (I.T.)
Mega Store

Bar
Cafe
Walkways
Semi-Covered Walkways
Event Plaza
Vided Wall & Signages

N

Jalan Pudu
Jalan Bukit Bintang
Jalan Imbi
Jalan Sultan Ismail

Basement Car Park
Restaurant Food

Basement level
land use

The Bukit Bintang Precinct is essentially one of urban place-making – a design which uses space between largely existing buildings,

Roof view

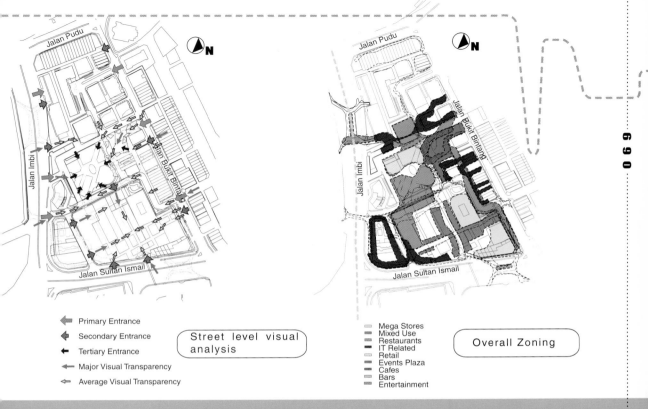

Street level visual analysis

◄ Primary Entrance
◄ Secondary Entrance
← Tertiary Entrance
← Major Visual Transparency
⇐ Average Visual Transparency

Overall Zoning

▭ Mega Stores
▬ Mixed Use
▭ Restaurants
▬ IT Related
▭ Retail
▭ Events Plaza
▭ Cafes
▭ Bars
▭ Entertainment

Aeriel View from Jalan Bukit Bintang

provides its own infill and is unified by an extensive, layered semi-enclosed canopy. The public precinct is thus defined by the roof, its structure and the freely placed organic forms which contain restaurants, cafes and food-kiosks, together with Retail outlets dispersed on the ground plane, with further restaurants and foodstalls at first floor – accessed by ramps and stairs.

The descending levels of the precinct to the south assist the ease of pedestrian transition in the long section to the upper level and street cross-over to Low Yat Plaza. The precinct will function both as retail centre and as a major public thoroughfare – for visitors it will provide a scenario which exhibits the Malaysian culture in both small-scale performances and an array of the local cuisine.

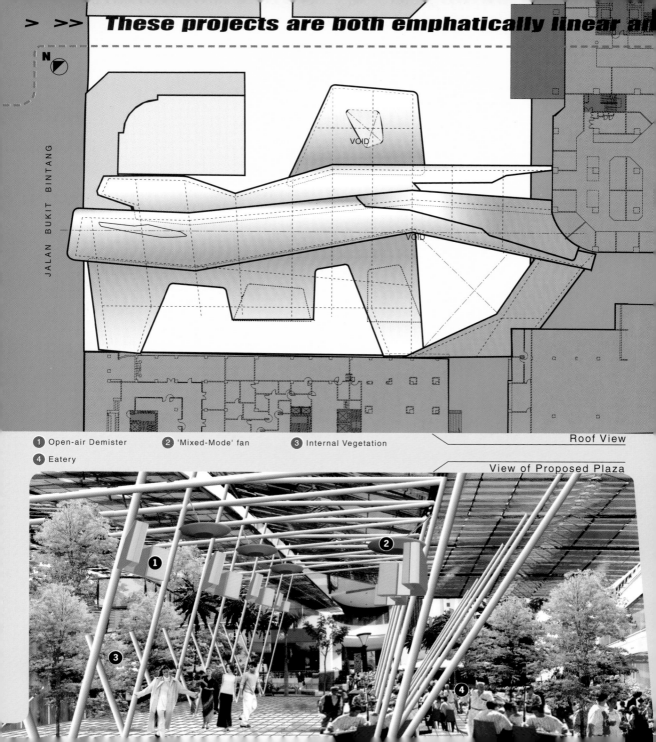

N

JALAN BUKIT BINTANG

VOID

VOID

Roof View

① Open-air Demister   ② 'Mixed-Mode' fan   ③ Internal Vegetation

④ Eatery

View of Proposed Plaza

bbpark

The flowing canopy-roof – Yeang's 'tropical umbrella' is a protective bioclimatic device on a huge scale. The canopy ha
secondary layers or 'leaves' of roofing, overlapped to permit cross-ventilation – these ventilation louvres and openabl
sliding roof panels enable cooling of the spaces below the roof, which coupled with overhead and demister fans kee
users cool and comfortable. Water features and landscaping further augment the comfort levels. The height of th
umbrella-canopy makes it a landmark structure and a focus for the whole community.

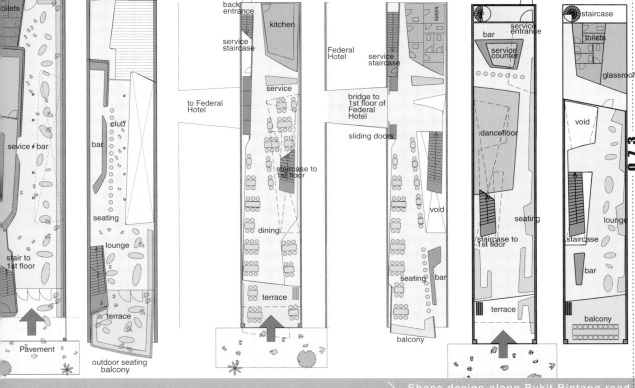

toilets

kitchen

back entrance

service staircase

sevice bar

service

to Federal Hotel

Federal Hotel

service staircase

club

bar

bridge to 1st floor of Federal Hotel

bar

seating

staircase to 1st floor

sliding doors

service counter

staircase

toilets

glassroof

dancefloor

void

void

lounge

stair to 1st floor

lounge

dining

seating

seating

staircase to 1st floor

staircase

bar

terrace

seating

bar

bar

Pavement

terrace

balcony

terrace

balcony

outdoor seating balcony

073

he structural steel masts support a steel frame and metal desk roof with poly carbonate sky heights. The masts also upport multi media screens, and it is intended to install super-bright lighting making 24-hour occupation a reality, rning 'night-into-day'. The simplicity of the bioclimatic design which relies entirely on the overall layered roof-umbrella and fan-driven air movement is Yeang's lightest and most economical creation, making new space in the public realm – an event in the tropical city.

之
城

er mei street

chinese opera

lion dance

ken + stephanie on site visit

mooncake festival

2.1 2.2 2.3 2.4 2.5 2.6 2.7 2.8 2.9 2.10 2.11 2.12 2

content page 1.11.21.3

May 1998 design

subscraper
taipei

四季地道之城

.14 2.15 2.16 2.17 2.18 2.19 2.20 2.21 2.22 2.23 2.24 2.25

3.1 3.2 3.3 credits

basement floors (underground project) no.sofstoreys taipei municipality Client 25.03°N Latitude Taipei, Taiwan Location ━ **Project Data** ━

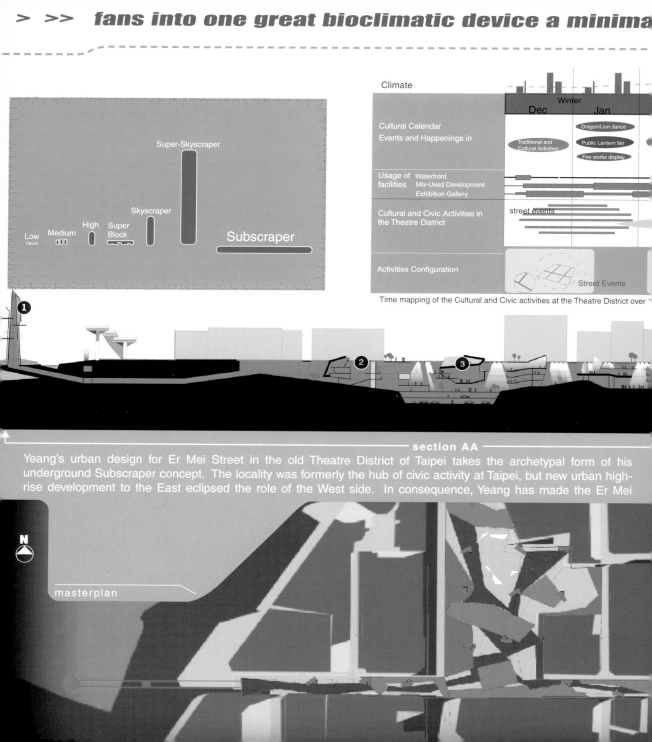

Climate

Cultural Calendar
Events and Happenings in

Winter
Dec   Jan

Traditional and Cultural Activities

Dragon/Lion dance
Public Lantern fair
Fire works display

Usage of facilities   Waterfront
    Mix-Used Development
    Exhibition Gallery

Cultural and Civic Activities in the Theatre District

street events

Activities Configuration

Street Events

Time mapping of the Cultural and Civic activities at the Theatre District over

Super-Skyscraper

Skyscraper

Subscraper

Low   Medium   High   Super Block

——— **section AA** ———

Yeang's urban design for Er Mei Street in the old Theatre District of Taipei takes the archetypal form of his underground Subscraper concept. The locality was formerly the hub of civic activity at Taipei, but new urban high-rise development to the East eclipsed the role of the West side. In consequence, Yeang has made the Er Mei

N

masterplan

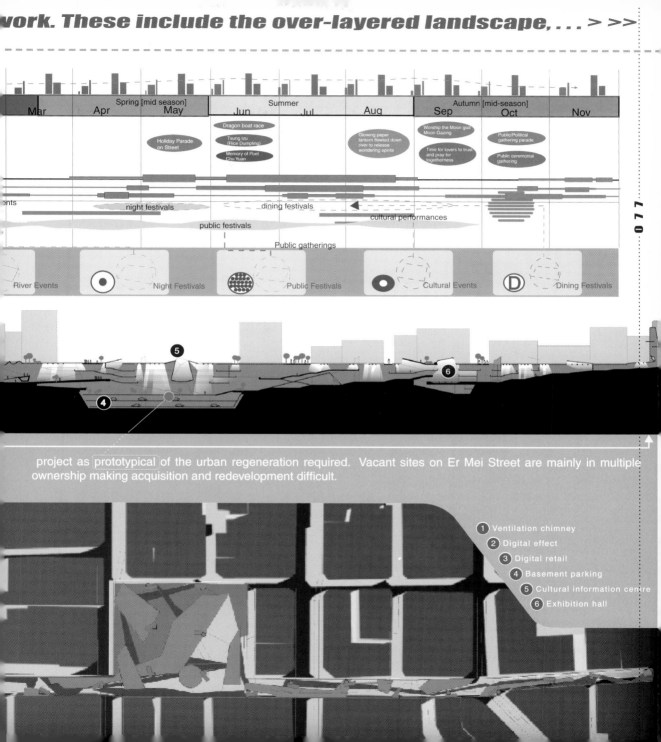

Mar	Apr	Spring [mid season] May	Jun	Summer Jul	Aug	Sep	Autumn [mid-season] Oct	Nov

Holiday Parade on Street

Dragon boat race

Tsung tzu (Rice Dumpling)

Memory of Poet Chu Yuan

Glowing paper lantern flowed down river to release wondering spirits

Worship the Moon god Moon Gazing

Time for lovers to trust and pray for togetherness

Public/Political gathering parade

Public ceremonial gathering

ents

night festivals

dining festivals

cultural performances

public festivals

Public gatherings

River Events   Night Festivals   Public Festivals   Cultural Events   Ⓓ Dining Festivals

④   ⑤   ⑥

project as ⟨prototypical⟩ of the urban regeneration required. Vacant sites on Er Mei Street are mainly in multiple ownership making acquisition and redevelopment difficult.

1 Ventilation chimney
2 Digital effect
3 Digital retail
4 Basement parking
5 Cultural information centre
6 Exhibition hall

Vertical Progression of Integration

Yeang's brilliant alternative solution was to use the entire street, which is public property, for regeneration and to pedestrianise and develop the street itself with a sunken development underground, using air-wells to bring light and ventilation into the deep spaces below. These spaces are occupied by a multitude of public

1. Outdoor Pavilion
2. Digital Retail
3. Digital Kiosk
4. I MAX Theatre
5. Amphitheatre
6. Science Gallery
7. 24hr Bookshop
8. Garden Pavilion
9. Floating Cafe
10. Digital Theme Park
11. Cultural Multi-Purpose Zone

Study model

Vertical Progression of Integration

079

and cultural facilities, together with retail areas, youth development center and linking pedestrian Promenade. The massive subscraper as it surfaces along the street level forms a great liner of forms, which in turn allows the existing buildings to be brought back into a new urban relationship.

Aerial View of Scheme

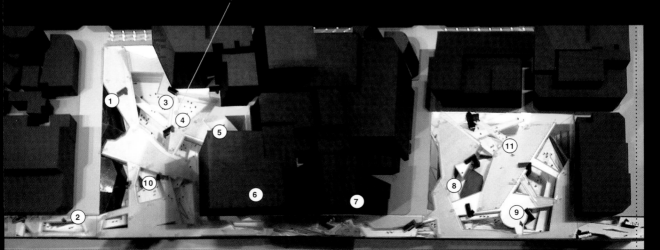

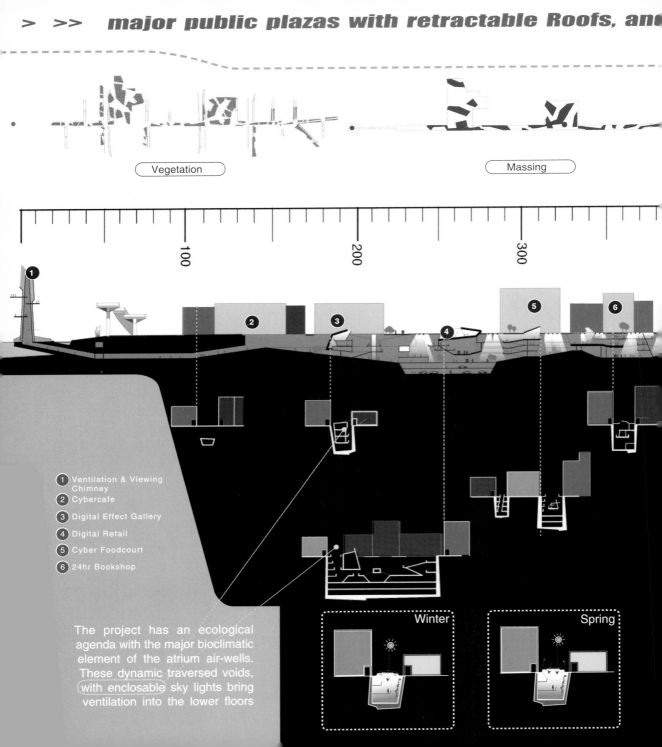

Vegetation

Massing

100   200   300

1 Ventilation & Viewing Chimney
2 Cybercafe
3 Digital Effect Gallery
4 Digital Retail
5 Cyber Foodcourt
6 24hr Bookshop

Winter   Spring

The project has an ecological agenda with the major bioclimatic element of the atrium air-wells. These dynamic traversed voids, with enclosable sky lights bring ventilation into the lower floors

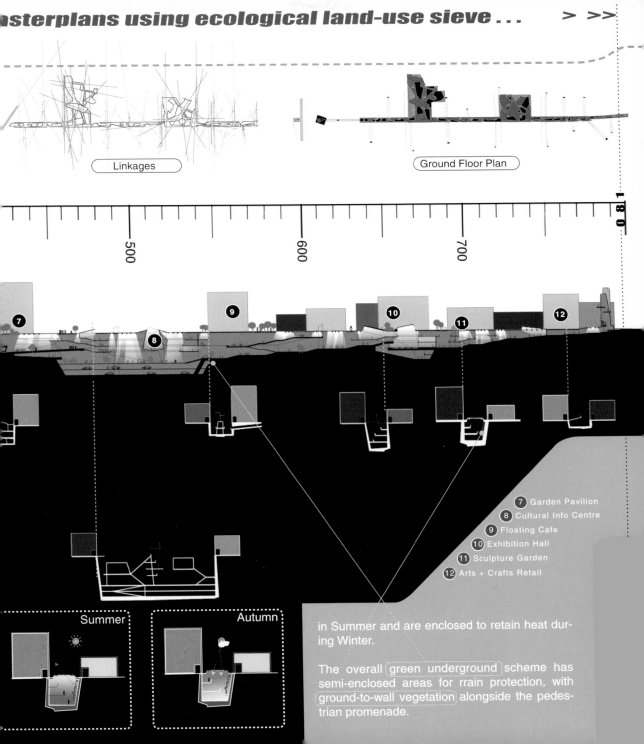

Linkages

Ground Floor Plan

500
600
700
0.8.1

7 Garden Pavilion
8 Cultural Info Centre
9 Floating Cafe
10 Exhibition Hall
11 Sculpture Garden
12 Arts + Crafts Retail

Summer

Autumn

in Summer and are enclosed to retain heat during Winter.

The overall green underground scheme has semi-enclosed areas for rrain protection, with ground-to-wall vegetation alongside the pedestrian promenade.

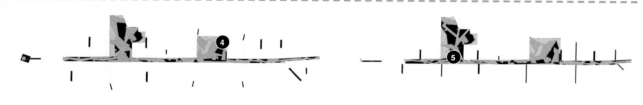

Level 01 Plan   Level 02 Plan

The singular big conceptual idea of the project is evident in the linear Site Plan, and in particular in the great alternated length of the Long-Section with its variable volumes, interconnected levels and air-well outcrops – the Urban Subscraper.

Cross-section of cultural multi-purpose zone

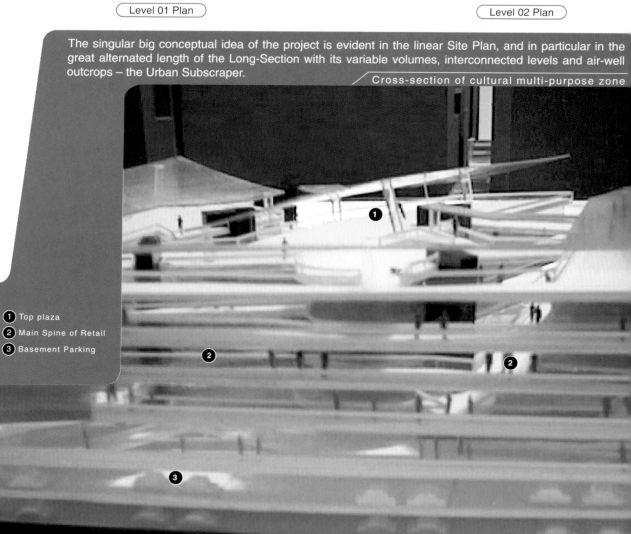

1. Top plaza
2. Main Spine of Retail
3. Basement Parking

Level 03 Plan

Level 04 Plan

④ Scattered Vertical Cones   ⑤ The Green Wall   ⑥ Multiple 'semi' covered platforms to create the underground city

North view of digital theme park

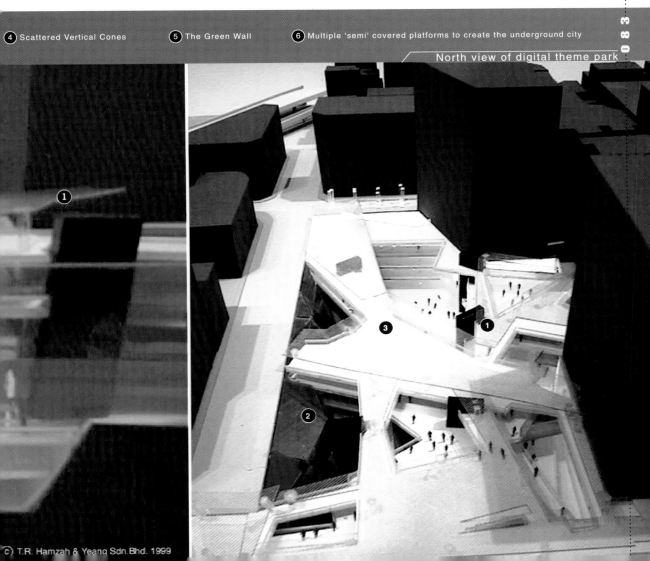

taichung civic

City Governement Building - gross: 140 120sq.m. City Council Building - gross: 63 343sq.m. Areas 18 storeys for both buildings no.sofstorey

center taiwan

2.14 2.15 2.16 2.17 2.18 2.19 2.20 2.21 2.22 2.23 2.24 2.25

3 13.2 3 3 credits

rg & Government, Taiwan, ROC Client The New Taichung City Civic Center District, Taichung, Taiwan Location —Project Data —

	Winter				Spring [Mid-Season]		Summ	
	December	January	February	March	April	May	June	July
Climate	48% 30%	50% 67% 22%	65% 37%	70% 37% 18%	57% 65%	41% 64%	52% 66% 43%	42%
Wind Direction & Speed								
Cultural Events	25 Constitution day	1-2 Founding day of The Republic of China 30 Lunar New Years Eve	1 Lunar New Year 1-15 Lantern Festival	29 Youth Day	4 Holiday for Women & Children 5 Tomb Sweeping Day	1 Labour Day	2 Dragon Boat Festival [Poet's day]	7-9. Summer V
Activities	• Traditional And Cultural Activities	• Dragon & Lion Dance • Performances • Folk Art Sale • Public Lantern Fair • Fire-works Display	• Holiday Parades On Streets			• Public Holiday Parades	• Dragon Boat Races • Tsung Tzu [Glutinous Rice Dumplings • Made in Memory of the Poet Chu Yuan	

Replaceable Structures		December	January	February	March	April	May	June	July
Fabric Canopies		☂	☂	☂ ☂ ☂	☂	☂	☂	☂	
Temporary Structures				〰 〰 〰	〰			〰	
Video Image Screens		▦		▦ ▦ ▦		▦	▦	▦ ▦ ▦ ▦	
Replaceable Pods		◖◗ ◖◗		◖◗	◖◗ ◖◗	◖◗ ◖◗	◖◗		●
Plug in Pods				◗ ◗					
Toilets & Services			⌐	⌐ ⌐	⌐ ⌐ ⌐	⌐ ⌐ ⌐	⌐ ⌐	⌐ ⌐	
Large Screens		大 大		大	大		大	大	
Lighting Projectors				⟜	⟜	⟜	⟜ ⟜	⟜ ⟜	
Pneumatic Structures				☁				☁	

The three major components of the Groundscraper are the City Council and Council Chamber building, the City Government building and a major multi-use Urban Plaza which is contained within a frame between the two major building forms.

As the brief emphasised the importance of culture, Yeang mapped the local cultural activities in relation to the four seasons of the year. These events are then temporarily housed in a series of changing canopies and replaceable structures, within the frame of the Plaza, to

Model Elevation

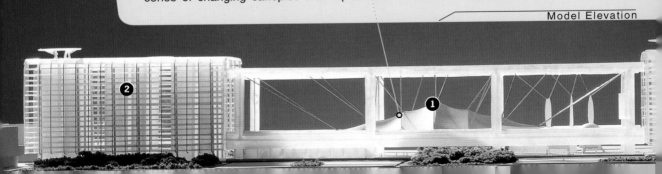

	Autumn [Mid-Season]		
August	September	October	November
hung Yuan stival host Month]	3 Armed Forces Day 9 Mid Autumn [Moon Festival] 28 Teachers Day Confucius Birthday	10 Double Tenth National Day	12 Taiwan's Retrocession Day 25 Dr Sun Yat-Sen's Birthday
g Paper Lanterns ated Down to Release ring Spirits	• Worship the Moon God • Moon Gazing • Time for Lovers to Trust • Pray for Togetherness	• Public/ Political Gathering/ Parade • Public Ceremonial Gathering	

Typical Level

Level 18

Level 07

Level 06

Level 05

Level 04

Level 03

Level 02

4 Level 01

To Carpark Level

5

City Council

Government Building

087

rovide an appro-
riate architecture
nd setting for each
easonal scenario
rising from the
ulture.

1 Main Plaza With Movable Fabric Structure   2 City Government Building   3 Council Chamber
4 To Government Building   5 To City Council

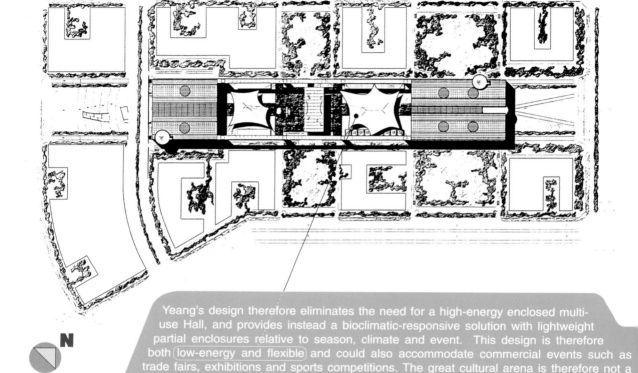

Yeang's design therefore eliminates the need for a high-energy enclosed multi-use Hall, and provides instead a bioclimatic-responsive solution with lightweight partial enclosures relative to season, climate and event. This design is therefore both low-energy and flexible and could also accommodate commercial events such as trade fairs, exhibitions and sports competitions. The great cultural arena is therefore not a formal building but an ecological space which frames and shelters the changing cultural pattern of its population. The major Groundscraper element is the massive linear space and frame that connects the two civic buildings.

Overall View of Model

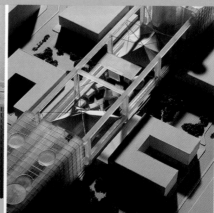

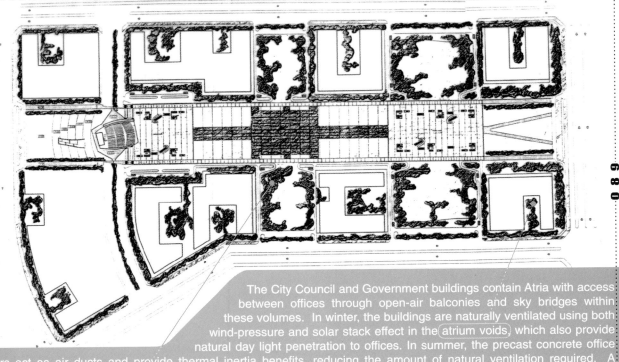

The City Council and Government buildings contain Atria with access between offices through open-air balconies and sky bridges within these volumes. In winter, the buildings are naturally ventilated using both wind-pressure and solar stack effect in the atrium voids, which also provide natural day light penetration to offices. In summer, the precast concrete office oors act as air ducts and provide thermal inertia benefits, reducing the amount of natural ventilation required. A entralised District cooling and Electrical Power Plant using clean agricultural fuels, distributes heating and cooling, ontributing to a sustainable environment. The two major civic frame are raised off the ground allowing the park land to ow underneath as a continuous landscape and incorporate extensive sunshading screen. Thus, Yeang's overall oncept is driven by major ecological principles embodied in the minimal-sheltered Cultural Plaza, contained by the two nd-forms of Atria-Office, configurations which together constitute the Taichung Civic Groundscraper.

Multiple Usage of the Cultural Plaza for the Change of Festivals and Seasons

lake club

'Rama-rama' (Butterfly)

3storeys with lower basementno.sofs

extension:

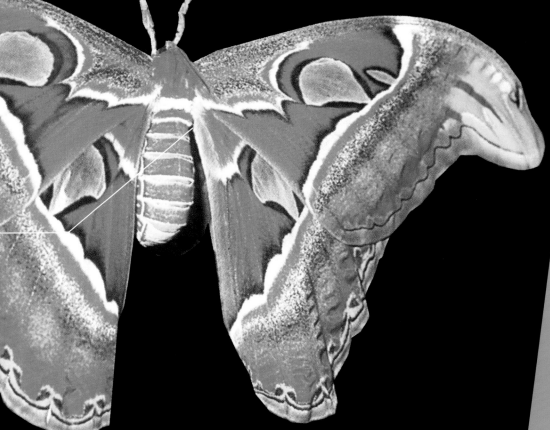

2.14 2.15 2.16 2.17 2.18 2.19 2.20 2.21 2.22 2.23 2.24 2.25

3.1 3.2 3.3 credits

Kelab Taman Perdana di Raja Client 101.40°E Longitude 2.9°N Latitude Lake Gardens, Kuala Lumpur Location ─ **Project Data** ─

Section

The design incorporates restaurants, banquet and multi-purpose halls as an underground extension of the club facilities, in a pristine park location, where the overall form is ventilated and daylit by a series of courtyards and wind-towers.

Yeang regards this is as the first of his Subscraper projects and the exploration of some basic principles, of this type.

These include the use of canopied staircases as a wind-conduit or tower, the waterfall atrium, and the 'Z'-louvered planting-channel roof form with continuous planting across the top of building. These elements are clearly expressed as forms, and in the roof and park plan respectively.

The wind-towers emerge as a series of garden pavilions punctuating the extended garden landscape. The landscape is retained and preserved and together with the use of water and the wind driven natural ventilation, the eco-systems of the project are brought into a sustainable balance.

Although relatively small and deliberately low-key, the project is a benchmark for the developments it signals in Yeang's ecological architecture, as it emerges in the 21st c entury.

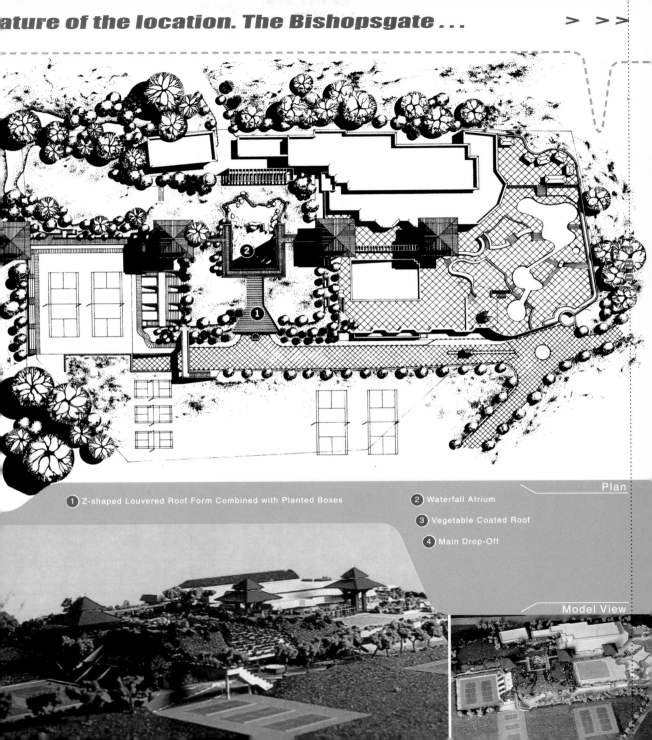

1 Z-shaped Louvered Roof Form Combined with Planted Boxes

2 Waterfall Atrium

3 Vegetable Coated Roof

4 Main Drop-Off

Plan

Model View

huanan new

masterplan & resid

Feng Shui Analysis by Jerry Too

2.14 2.15 2.16 2.17 2.18 2.19 2.20 2.21 2.25 2.23 2.24 2.25

3.13.2 3.3 creating

city :
ential township
guangzhou

12storeys no.sofstoreys 500acres Site Area Hopson Development Holdings Ltd.Client Guangzhou, China Location — Project Data —

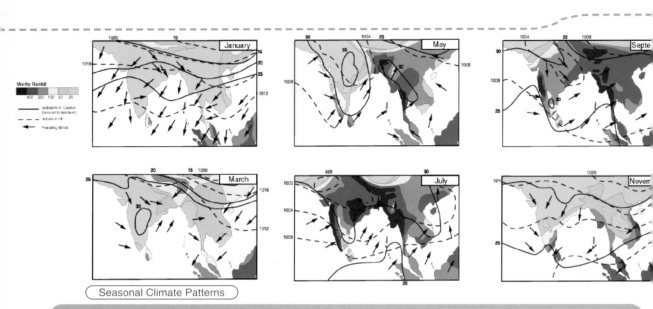

Seasonal Climate Patterns

The masterplan is for a Residential-based township with a full range of public and commercial facilities, transportation links and public open spaces for all aspects of leisure and family life. The major natural features of the 498 acre site are its major (northern frontage) to the Pearl River, and the (natural hillocks) within the agricultural landform.

View of model and main hillocks

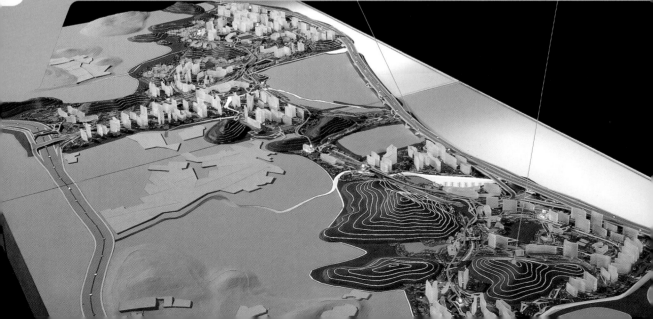

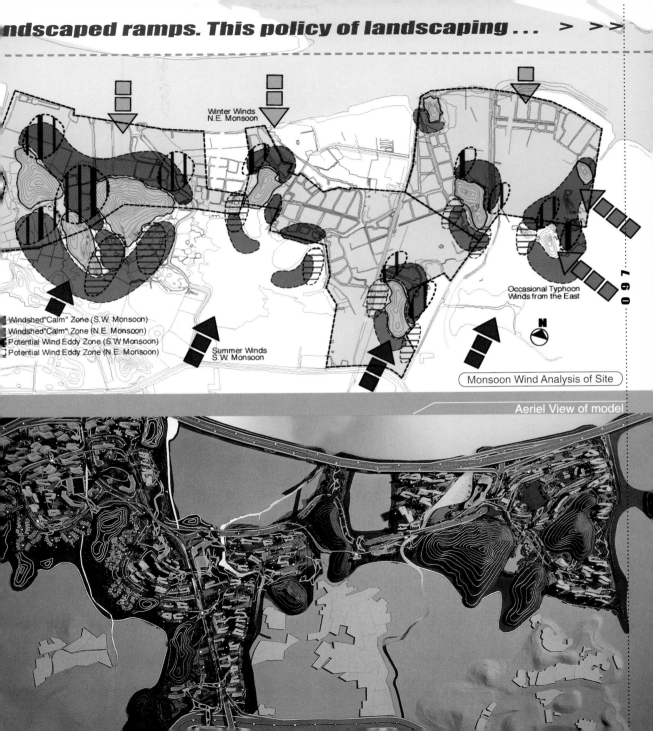

Winter Winds
N.E. Monsoon

Windshed "Calm" Zone (S.W. Monsoon)
Windshed "Calm" Zone (N.E. Monsoon)
Potential Wind Eddy Zone (S.W. Monsoon)
Potential Wind Eddy Zone (N.E. Monsoon)

Summer Winds
S.W. Monsoon

Occasional Typhoon
Winds from the East

N

Monsoon Wind Analysis of Site

Aeriel View of model

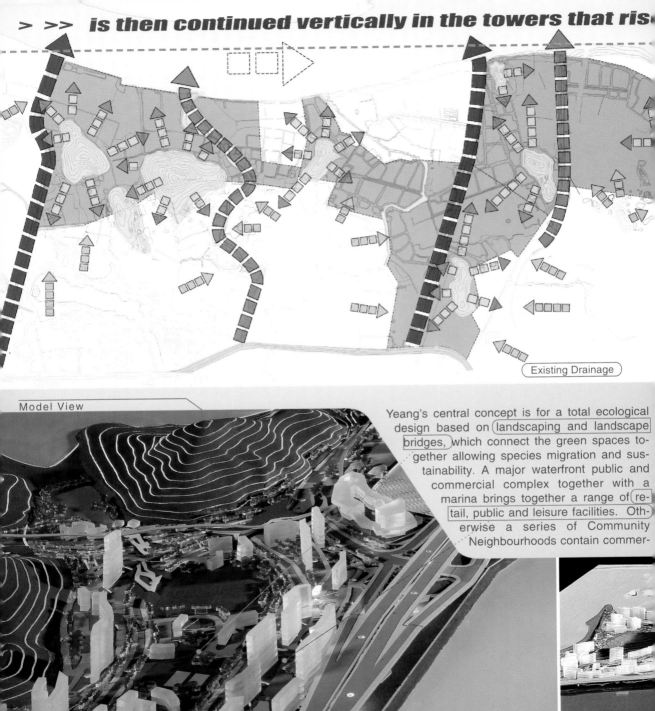

Existing Drainage

Model View

Yeang's central concept is for a total ecological design based on landscaping and landscape bridges, which connect the green spaces together allowing species migration and sustainability. A major waterfront public and commercial complex together with a marina brings together a range of retail, public and leisure facilities. Otherwise a series of Community Neighbourhoods contain commer-

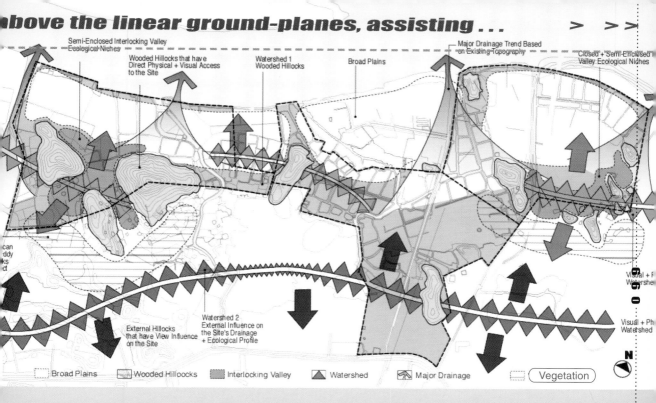

Semi-Enclosed Interlocking Valley Ecological Niches

Wooded Hillocks that have Direct Physical + Visual Access to the Site

Watershed 1 Wooded Hillocks

Broad Plains

Major Drainage Trend Based on Existing Topography

Closed + Semi-Enclosed Valley Ecological Niches

Visual + P Watershe

Visual + Ph Watershed

External Hillocks that have View Influence on the Site

Watershed 2 External Influence on the Site's Drainage + Ecological Profile

N

Broad Plains   Wooded Hilloocks   Interlocking Valley   Watershed   Major Drainage   Vegetation

cial and recreational or educational facilities together with (High-rise Courtyard Apartments) or 2 storey modern "Chinese" Courtyard Houses in rows. The concept of continuous landscaping and green belts from the natural hillocks through to the river's edge also forms a backdrop to the houses and apartments and provides landscape views. The communities are threaded together with pedestrian walkways separate from the main tree-lined traffic boulevards and avenues. The high-rise apartments generally orientated north-south, are centred on the principle of a courtyard, increasing natural light and ventilation to the living areas. The bioclimatic design resembles Yeang's MBf Apartment Tower in Penang, in this case with natural shading from the courtyard overhangs which are also fitted with folding, louvered external shutters.   Characteristically, landscaped sky-courts are placed at the higher levels for communal use by residents. The low-rise modern Courtyard Houses arranged in rows and generally around the valleys of the natural hillocks are Yeang's version of a Chinese Court-House. The innovative plans incorporate an open terrace on

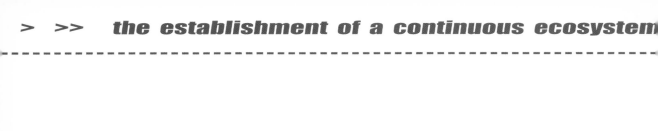

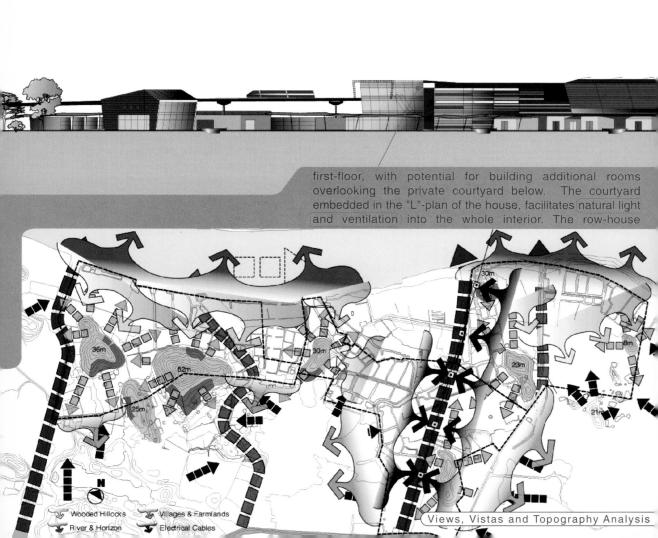

first-floor, with potential for building additional rooms overlooking the private courtyard below. The courtyard embedded in the "L"-plan of the house, facilitates natural light and ventilation into the whole interior. The row-house

36m

62m

30m

30m

23m

25m

8m

21

N

Wooded Hillocks   Villages & Farmlands

River & Horizon   Electrical Cables

Views, Vistas and Topography Analysis

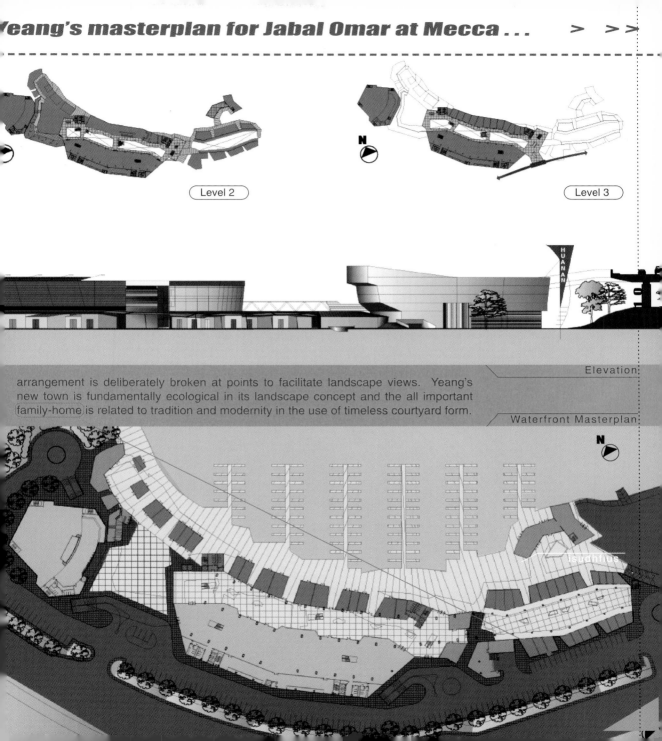

Level 2

N

Level 3

Elevation

Waterfront Masterplan

N

arrangement is deliberately broken at points to facilitate landscape views. Yeang's new town is fundamentally ecological in its landscape concept and the all important family-home is related to tradition and modernity in the use of timeless courtyard form.

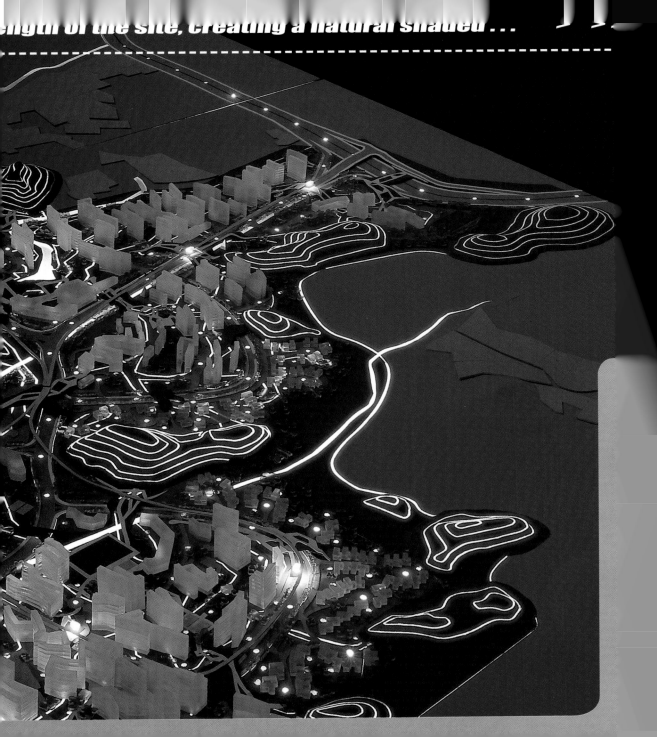

PLA western

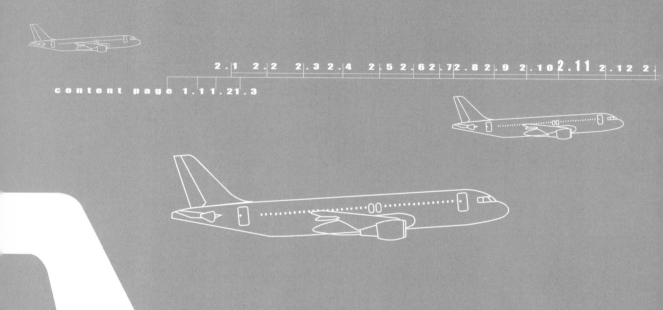

development
phase two

.14 2.15 2.16 2.17 2.18 2.19 2.20 2.21 2.22 2.23 2.24 2.25

3.1 3.2 3.3 credits

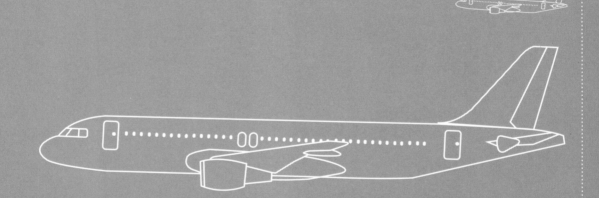

0m2 Site Area gross:110 113m2 areas 6storeys no.ofstoreys Singapore Aviation Client 1.22˚ N Latitude Singapore Location **— Project Data —**

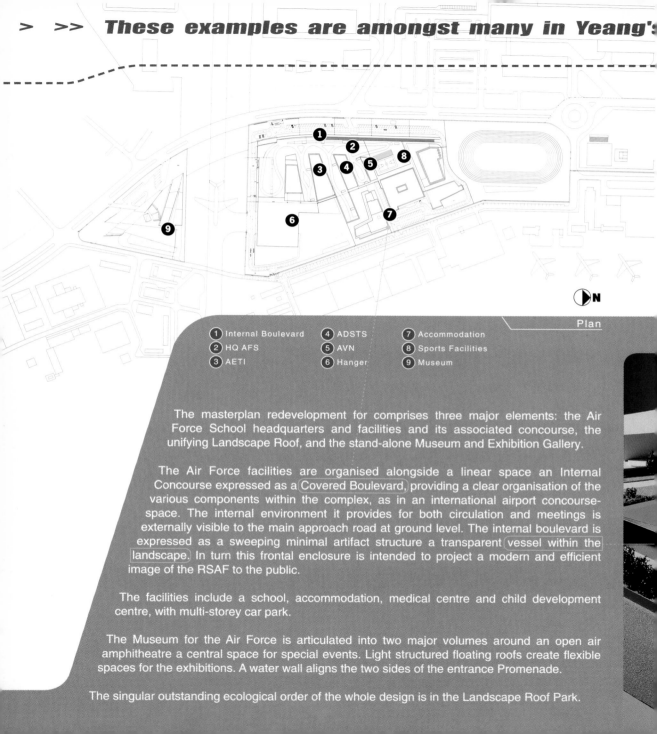

N

Plan

1. Internal Boulevard
2. HQ AFS
3. AETI
4. ADSTS
5. AVN
6. Hanger
7. Accommodation
8. Sports Facilities
9. Museum

The masterplan redevelopment for comprises three major elements: the Air Force School headquarters and facilities and its associated concourse, the unifying Landscape Roof, and the stand-alone Museum and Exhibition Gallery.

The Air Force facilities are organised alongside a linear space an Internal Concourse expressed as a Covered Boulevard, providing a clear organisation of the various components within the complex, as in an international airport concourse-space. The internal environment it provides for both circulation and meetings is externally visible to the main approach road at ground level. The internal boulevard is expressed as a sweeping minimal artifact structure a transparent vessel within the landscape. In turn this frontal enclosure is intended to project a modern and efficient image of the RSAF to the public.

The facilities include a school, accommodation, medical centre and child development centre, with multi-storey car park.

The Museum for the Air Force is articulated into two major volumes around an open air amphitheatre a central space for special events. Light structured floating roofs create flexible spaces for the exhibitions. A water wall aligns the two sides of the entrance Promenade.

The singular outstanding ecological order of the whole design is in the Landscape Roof Park.

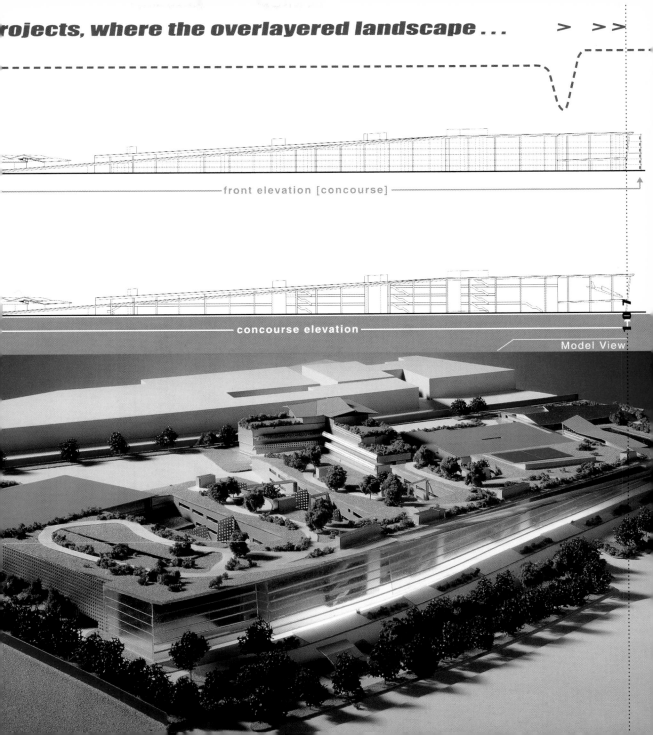

rojects, where the overlayered landscape ...   > >>

front elevation [concourse]

concourse elevation

Model View

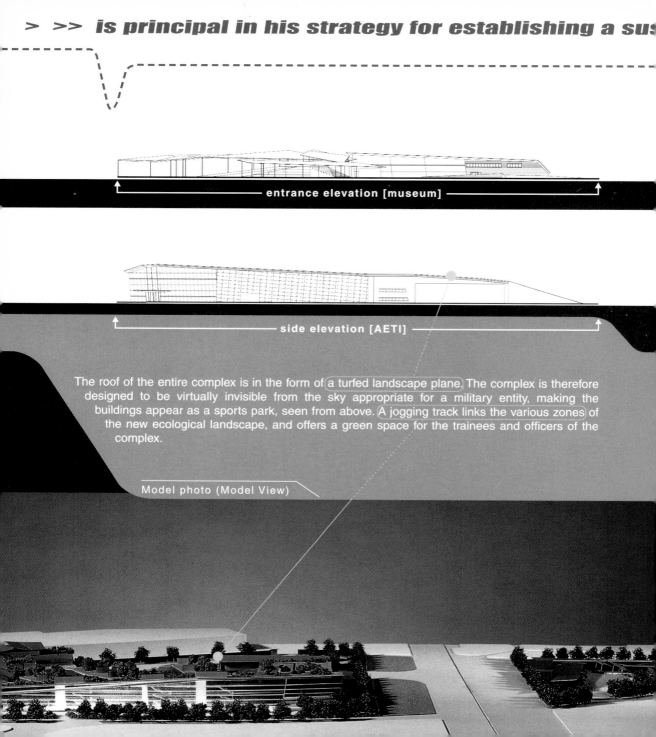

entrance elevation [museum]

side elevation [AETI]

The roof of the entire complex is in the form of a turfed landscape plane. The complex is therefore designed to be virtually invisible from the sky appropriate for a military entity, making the buildings appear as a sports park, seen from above. A jogging track links the various zones of the new ecological landscape, and offers a green space for the trainees and officers of the complex.

Model photo (Model View)

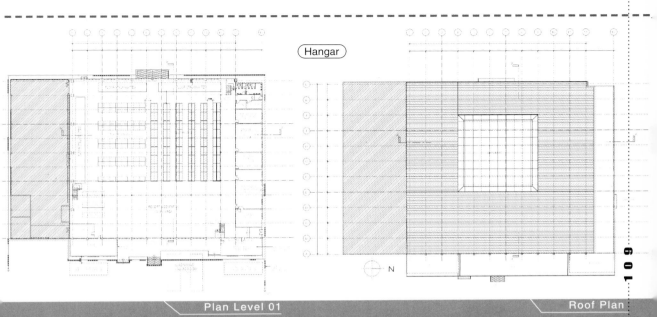

Hangar

Plan Level 01

Roof Plan

N

This singular commitment of the design to major landscape restoration, within the semi-industrial nature of the location, accords with Yeang's first principles of introducing stability and sustainability to the overall eco-systems of the site.

Model View

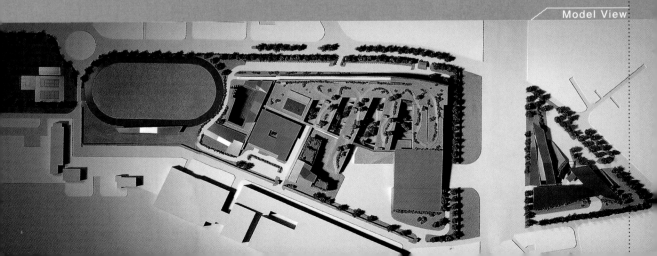

telekom mul
univer

C[41.6%] + M[14.1%] + Y[3.5%] + K[0.4%]

C[33.33%] + M[60.78%] + Y[62.8%] + K[25.9%]

.14 | 2.15 | 2.16 | 2.17 | 2.18 | 2.19 | 2.20 | 2.21 | 2.22 | 2.23 | 2.24 | 2.25

3.1 | 3.2 | 3.3 c r e d i t s

timedia
sity : malaysia

C[18%] + M[15%] + Y[0%] + K[40%]

res SiteArea 2.5millionsq.ft.Areas Telekom MalaysiaClient 101.40°ELongitude 3.20°N Latitude Cyberjaya,Malaysia Location **— Project Data —**

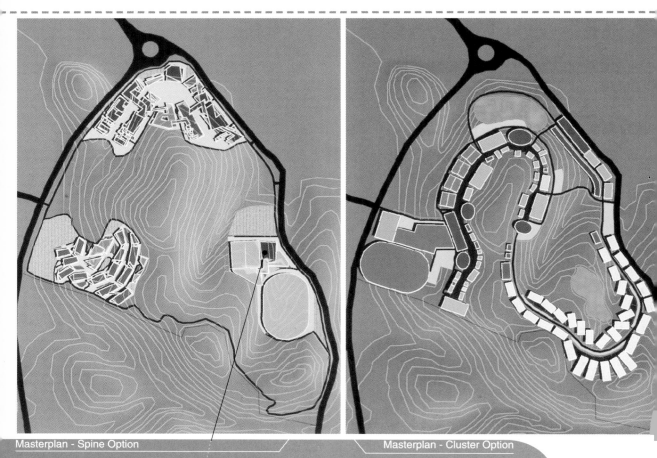

Masterplan - Spine Option

Masterplan - Cluster Option

The University is sited within the Multimedia Super Corridor of Cyberjaya, and the design aims to establish a State-of-the-Art Multimedia University. The teaching and monitoring systems use multimedia and digital technology for communication, information retrieval and transactions. The Auditoria are designed as a TV studio, with mini-workstations and lectures are delivered by electronic media, and not by repetitive personal presentation from lecturers. Instead, emphasis is placed on workshops in a return to traditional master-apprentice one-to-one tutorials and evaluation.

Yeang's overall Masterplan Concept is a generic solution with a low environmental impact layout. A series of Masterplan options are then developed and related to an intensive ecological survey of the site and its natural features. These options include The Hub an urban concept, The Villages and The Promenade both more dispersed. The latter reflects something of Yeang's Malaysian University of Nottingham and is the most organically-wound into the topography, with two major lakes. The Faculty structure and associated facilities, including student Residential accommodation is common to all the proposals.

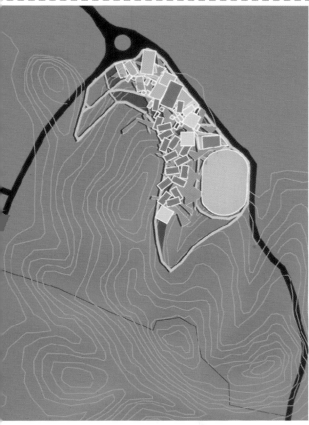

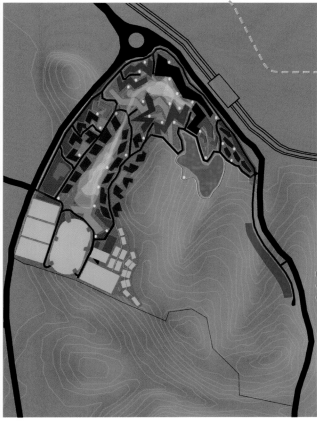

Masterplan - Final Option

Close-up shot of options [directly above]   Masterplan - Hub Option [above left]

side from the unusually varied and comprehensive masterplanning options, each developed in some detail, Yeang's host important method statement for the project is both ecological and characteristically precise.

e establishes clearly that ecological or green design for large sites should start with a mapping analysis of the eco-

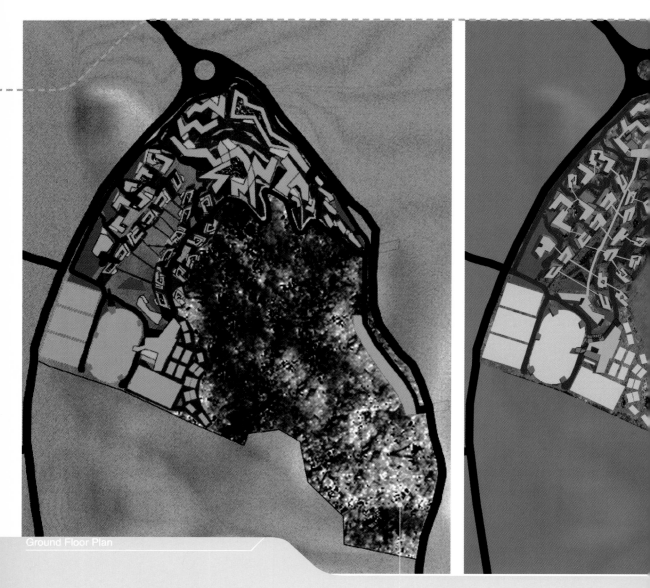

Ground Floor Plan

-system and a study of the ecological constraints of the locality.

Yeang's objectives, within this mapping exercise, are to identify the ecological carrying capacity of the site, which then enables him as the designer to locate built structures, access roads and circulation systems in a way that minimizes their impact on the ecosystem's functioning and wherever possible, maximizes environmental productivity. A technique that is commonly used is that of ecological land-use sieve-mapping which incorporates site topography,

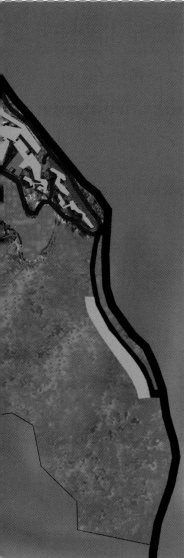

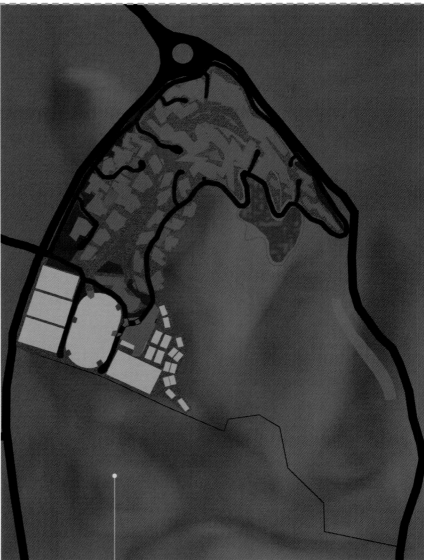

115

Typical Floor

Roof Plan

A technique that is commonly used is that of ecological land-use sieve-mapping which incorporates site topography, slope analysis, topographical analysis, drainage, access and visual analysis. In the case of the Multimedia University, Yeang used a simplified version of the mapping technique, that was limited by incomplete ecological data.

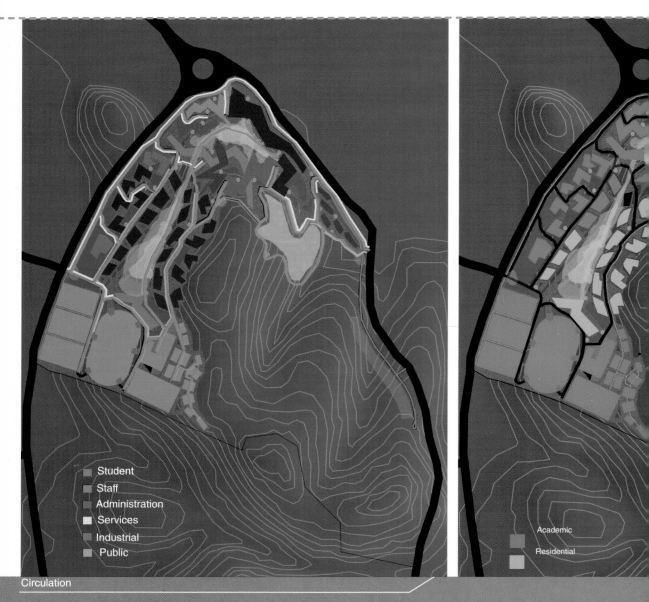

Student
Staff
Administration
Services
Industrial
Public

Academic

Residential

Circulation

Nevertheless, as an outline design with optional variants, it is both sensitive to and ecologically-integrated with
natural setting.

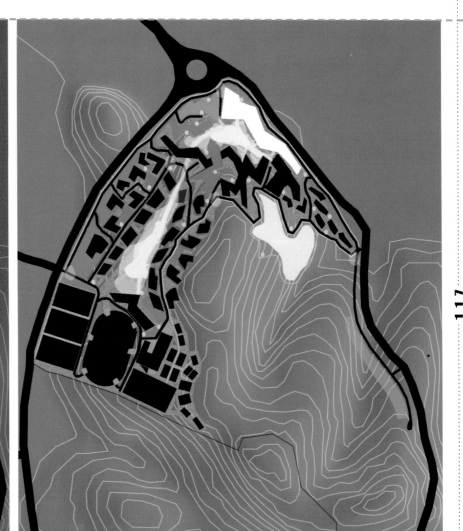

Phasing

Zoning

WIPO

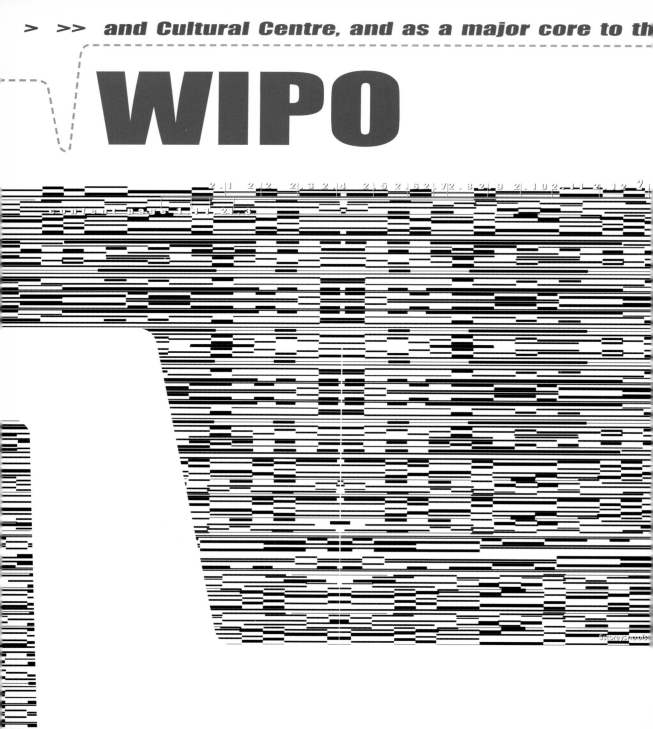

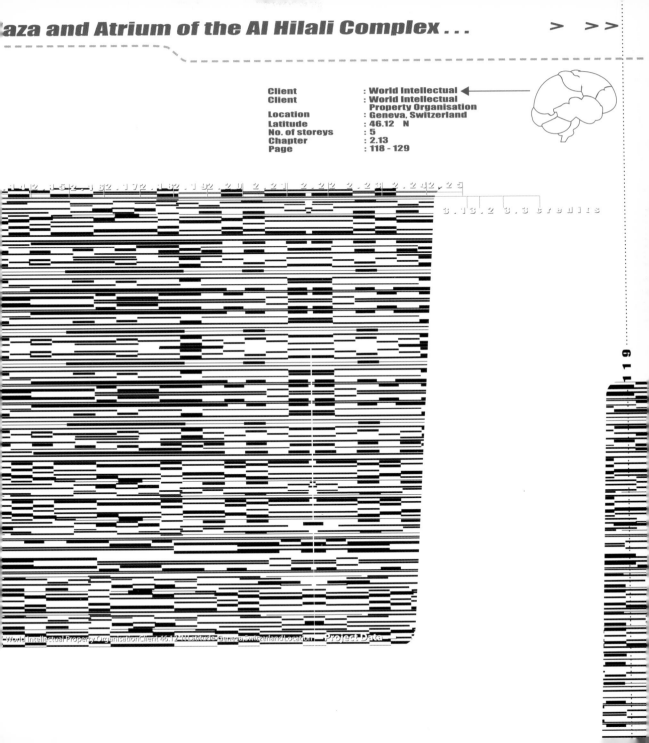

Client	: World Intellectual
Client	: World Intellectual Property Organisation
Location	: Geneva, Switzerland
Latitude	: 46.12 N
No. of storeys	: 5
Chapter	: 2.13
Page	: 118 – 129

World Intellectual Property OrganisationClient 46.12 N Latitude Geneva Switzerland Location **Project Data**

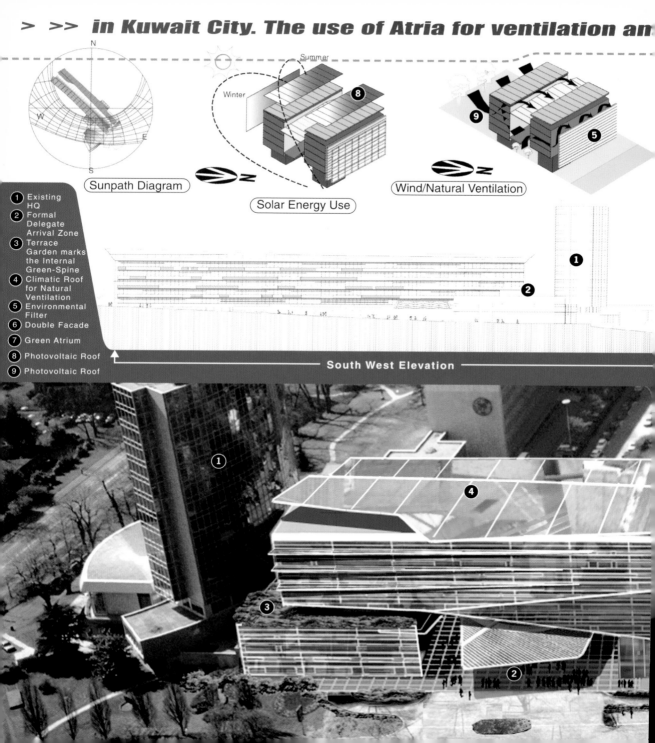

Sunpath Diagram

Solar Energy Use

Winter

Summer

Wind/Natural Ventilation

1. Existing HQ
2. Formal Delegate Arrival Zone
3. Terrace Garden marks the Internal Green-Spine
4. Climatic Roof for Natural Ventilation
5. Environmental Filter
6. Double Facade
7. Green Atrium
8. Photovoltaic Roof
9. Photovoltaic Roof

South West Elevation

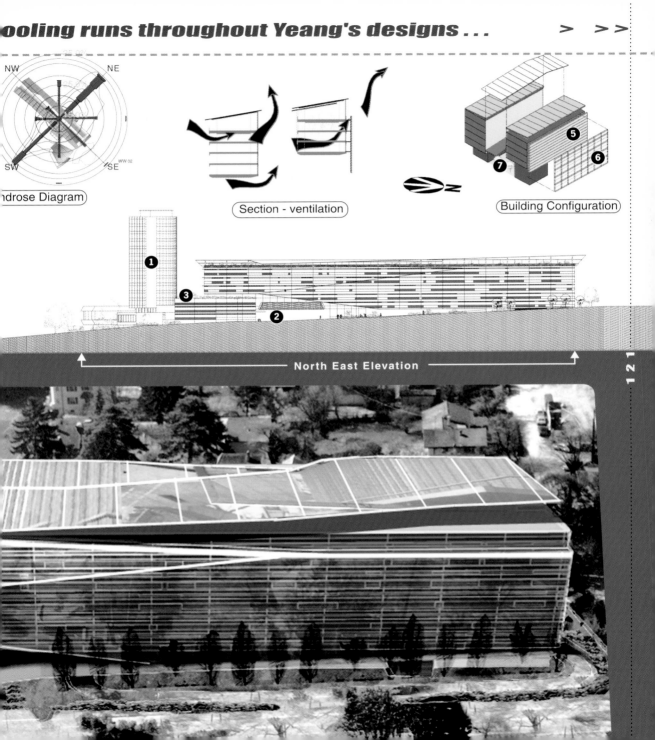

NW   NE

SW   SE   WW 02

ndrose Diagram

Section - ventilation

Building Configuration

❶

❸

❷

❺

❼

❻

North East Elevation

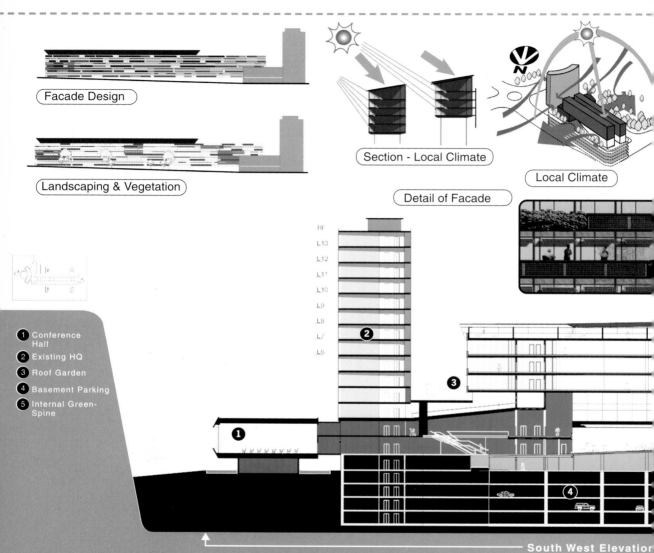

Facade Design

Landscaping & Vegetation

Section - Local Climate

Local Climate

Detail of Facade

1 Conference Hall
2 Existing HQ
3 Roof Garden
4 Basement Parking
5 Internal Green-Spine

RF
L13
L12
L11
L10
L9
L8
L7
L6

South West Elevation

The design objective that Yeang has established for the WIPO project is to create a world-class state-of-the-art building of excellence which fully responds to the WIPO brief requirements, and is at the same time an ecologically-sustainable low-energy and   design. The general form of the overall solution consists of a major new conference hall hub, that adjoins the existing tower, with main entrance and foyer. The remainder of the new office accommodation which can be flexibly arranged, is contained in a north-western linear extension with a central atrium, both alongside the Route de Ferney, and facing into the gardens on the quieter southern side of the site.

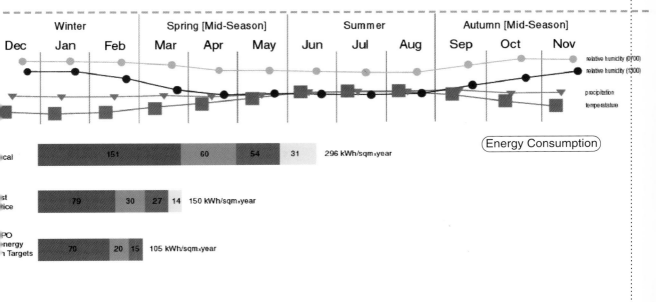

	Winter			Spring [Mid-Season]			Summer			Autumn [Mid-Season]		
Dec	Jan	Feb	Mar	Apr	May	Jun	Jul	Aug	Sep	Oct	Nov

relative humidity (0700)
relative humidity (1300)
precipitation
temperature

(Energy Consumption)

ical — 151 | 60 | 54 | 31 — 296 kWh/sqm×year

st tice — 79 | 30 | 27 | 14 — 150 kWh/sqm×year

PO nergy n Targets — 70 | 20 | 15 — 105 kWh/sqm×year

5

L5
L4
L3
L2
L1
L0
L-1
L-2
L-3
L-4
L-5

1 2 3

Servicing and carparking are located in basement floors and servicing ramps, together with main entrance and semi-covered porte-cochère are both accessed from the Route de Ferney frontage. The openness of the ground level linkage, at the main entrance, also allows residential occupants of adjacent properties to pass through the portal of the new building.

Yeang's design is exceptionally well engineered in its security arrangements for conference delegates, staff and visitors with separation and distinct controls. The spatial concept of hub and linear-arm is also designed to deliver a legible, coherent form immediately comprehensible to all users.

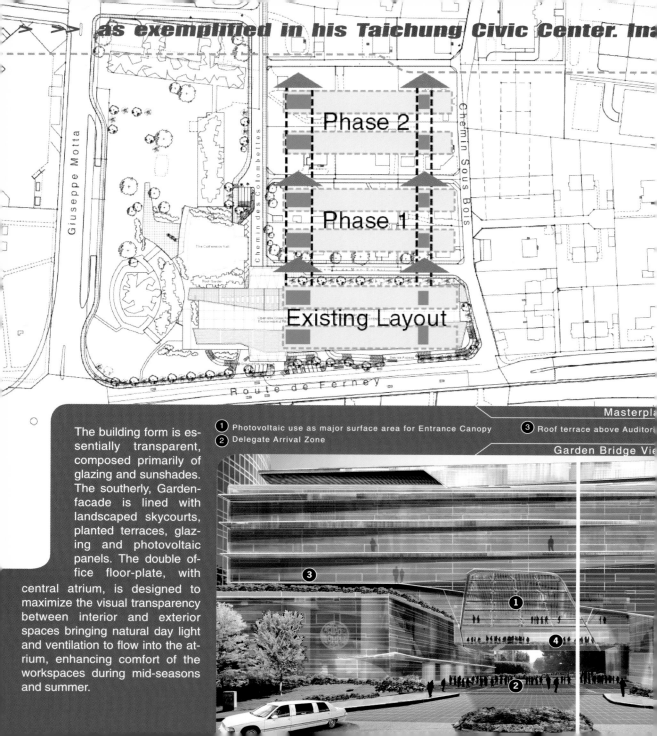

Phase 2

Phase 1

Existing Layout

Giuseppe Motta

Chemin des Colombettes

Chemin Sous Bois

Route de Ferney

Masterpla

① Photovoltaic use as major surface area for Entrance Canopy
② Delegate Arrival Zone
③ Roof terrace above Auditori

Garden Bridge Vie

The building form is essentially transparent, composed primarily of glazing and sunshades. The southerly, Garden-facade is lined with landscaped skycourts, planted terraces, glazing and photovoltaic panels. The double office floor-plate, with central atrium, is designed to maximize the visual transparency between interior and exterior spaces bringing natural day light and ventilation to flow into the atrium, enhancing comfort of the workspaces during mid-seasons and summer.

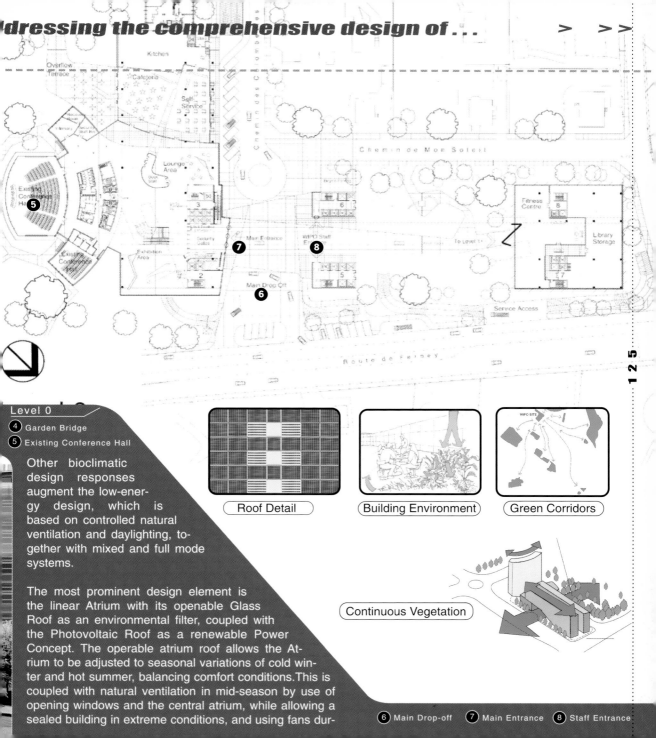

Kitchen

Overflow Terrace

Cafeteria

Self Service

Lounge Area

Existing Conference Hall **5**

Existing Conference Hall

Security Office

Exhibition Area

7 Main Entrance

6 Main Drop Off

8 WIPO Staff Entrance

Chemin de Mon Soleil

To Level 1

Fitness Centre

Library Storage

Service Access

Route de Ferney

1 2 5

Other bioclimatic design responses augment the low-energy design, which is based on controlled natural ventilation and daylighting, together with mixed and full mode systems.

The most prominent design element is the linear Atrium with its openable Glass Roof as an environmental filter, coupled with the Photovoltaic Roof as a renewable Power Concept. The operable atrium roof allows the Atrium to be adjusted to seasonal variations of cold winter and hot summer, balancing comfort conditions. This is coupled with natural ventilation in mid-season by use of opening windows and the central atrium, while allowing a sealed building in extreme conditions, and using fans dur-

(Roof Detail)

(Building Environment)

(Green Corridors)

(Continuous Vegetation)

WIPO SITE

6 Main Drop-off   **7** Main Entrance   **8** Staff Entrance

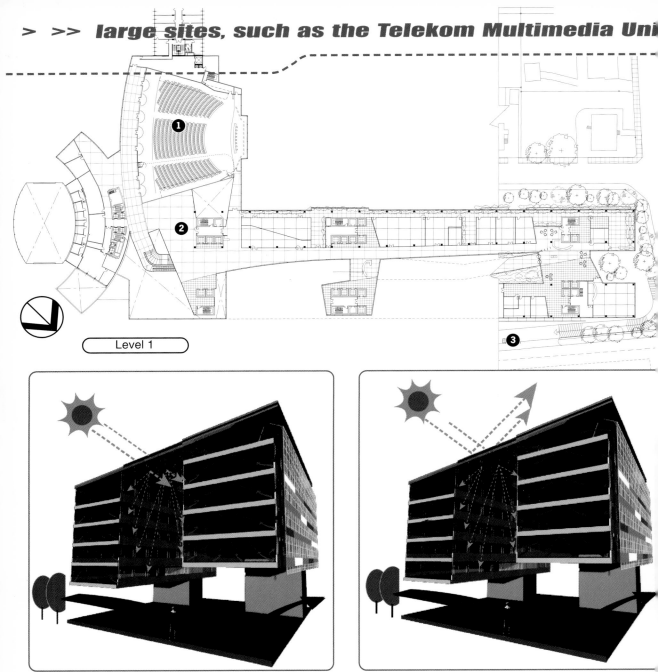

Level 1

Seasonal Operation - Summer

Seasonal Operation - Mid Seaso

ing summer to circulate coolth stored in the structure. Conversely recovered exhaust air heat can be circulated in winter periods. Taken together with fully integrated M&E and IT systems, the whole design is a bioclimatic machine à habiter. It extends the pioneering tradition in Geneva's contemporary architecture, established by Le Cor-

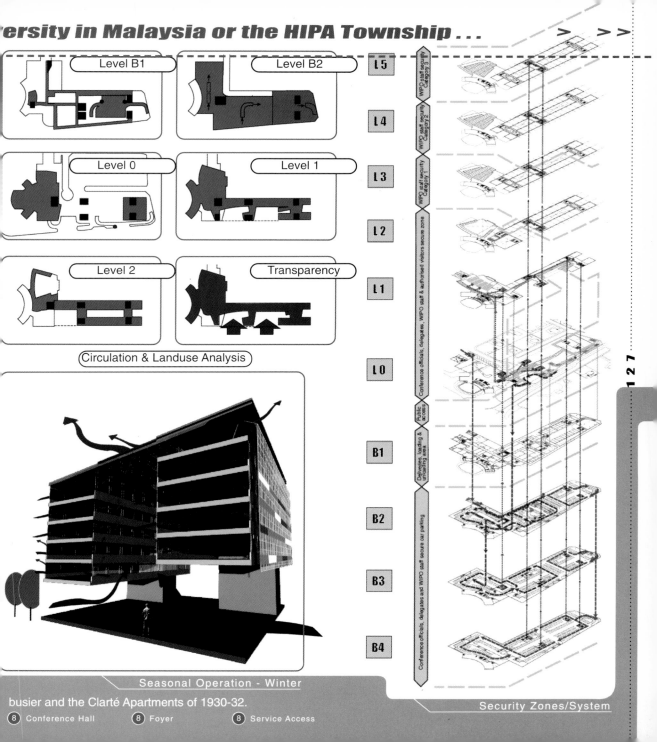

Level B1

Level B2

Level 0

Level 1

Level 2

Transparency

Circulation & Landuse Analysis

L5

L4

L3

L2

L1

L0

B1

B2

B3

B4

WIPO staff security Category 3

WIPO staff security Category 2

WIPO staff security Category 1

Conference officials, delegates, WIPO staff & authorised visitors secure zone

Public access

Deliveries, loading & unloading area

Conference officials, delegates and WIPO staff secure car parking

Seasonal Operation - Winter

Security Zones/System

busier and the Clarté Apartments of 1930-32.

(8) Conference Hall   (8) Foyer   (8) Service Access

1 Existing
HQ
2 Existing
Conference
Hall
3 Canopy
Entrance
4 Auditorium

content page 1.1 1.2 1.3

2.1 2.2 2.3 2.4 2.5 2.6 2.7 2.8 2.9 2.10 2.11 2.12 2.1

tianjin civil school

'Flugzeug' (Plane)

March 1998 Completion January 1998 Date start 6 storeys no. of storeys 333 000 sq.m Sit

14

aviation
:china

48 137sq.m. gross: 191 921sq.m. Areas Commanding HQ of China School Client 39.72°N Latitude Tianjin, China Location —**Project Data** —

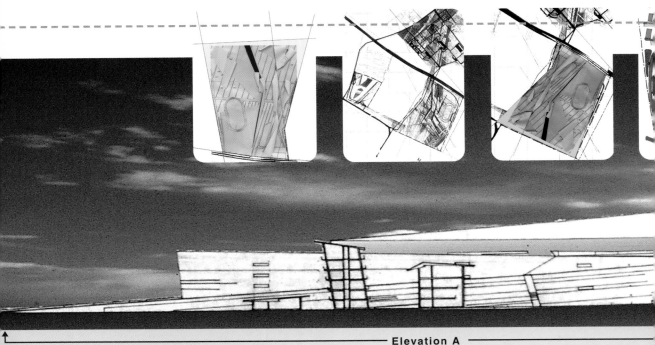

— **Elevation A** —

The masterplan of the complex is derived from the Chinese character O IO (human) and is translated into a skewed planar-geometric series of Walls which govern the pedestrian circulation. The figurative wall-planes divide the site into 3 secure zones: Sports facilities, Student Residential accommodation and Academic facilities.

Main Entrance to Campus

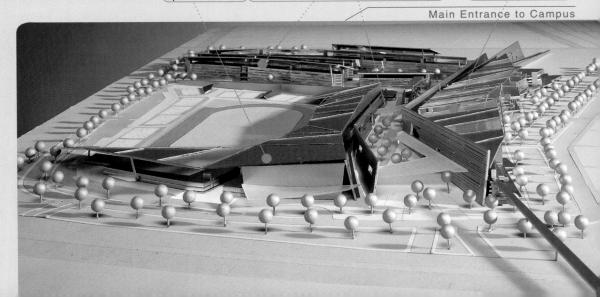

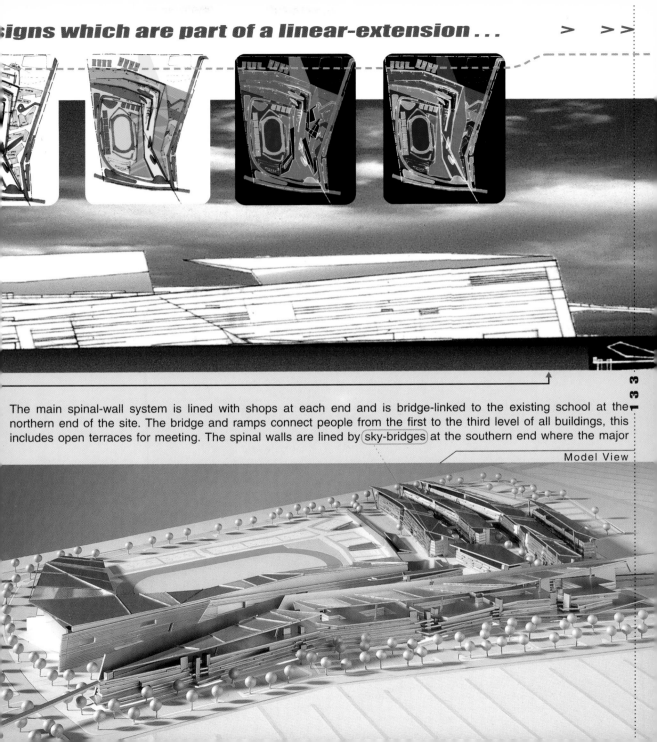

The main spinal-wall system is lined with shops at each end and is bridge-linked to the existing school at the northern end of the site. The bridge and ramps connect people from the first to the third level of all buildings, this includes open terraces for meeting. The spinal walls are lined by sky-bridges at the southern end where the major

Model View

— ↑ — **Elevation B** —

confluence of academic and residential space occurs. Seen from overhead two outstanding features are evident: the planar-geometric Walls governing the arrangement and defining the Central concourse, and the tilted roof planes - orientated north-south. Yeang claims that overall roof form can be read as a series of wings, an image that recalls the form of the Stealth fighter aircraft.

Model View

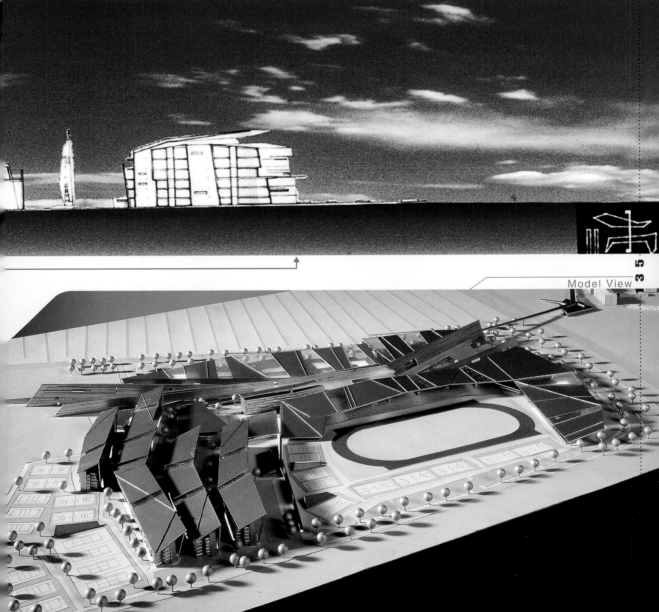

Model View

> >> the functioning of the eco-system. Similar charac

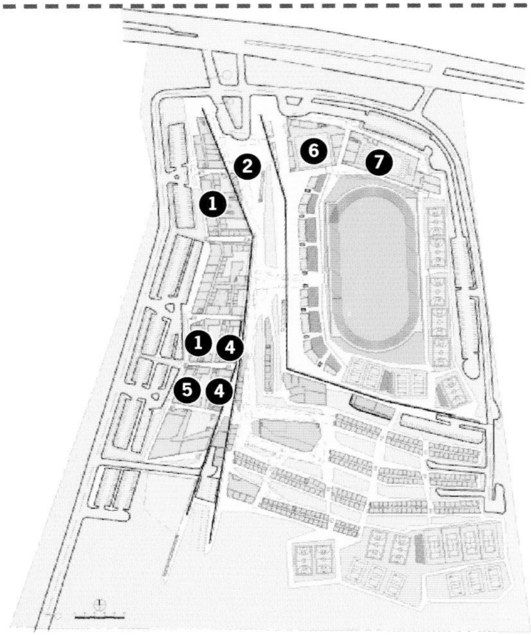
1
2
6
7
1
4
5
4

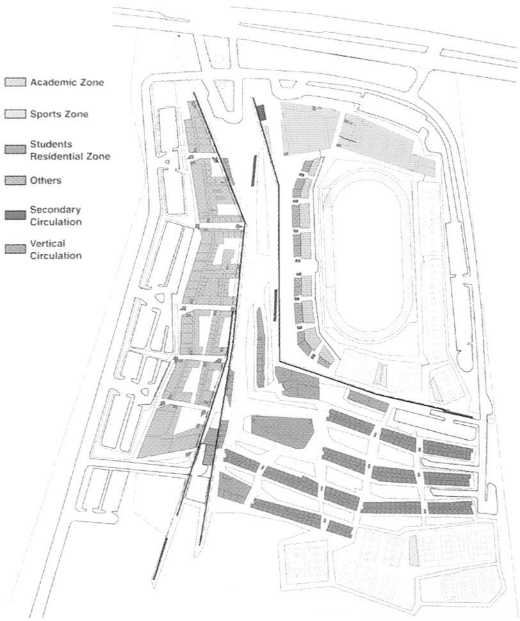
Academic Zone
Sports Zone
Students Residential Zone
Others
Secondary Circulation
Vertical Circulation

But, the overriding importance of the roof form is the bioclimatic function it performs: the accommodation is north-south orientated-this maximises the buildings_ exposure to solar gain from the low-setting winter sun. Sun louvres are

1. Business Centre
2. Shops
3. Library
4. Computer Centre
5. Science Centre
6. Sports Hall

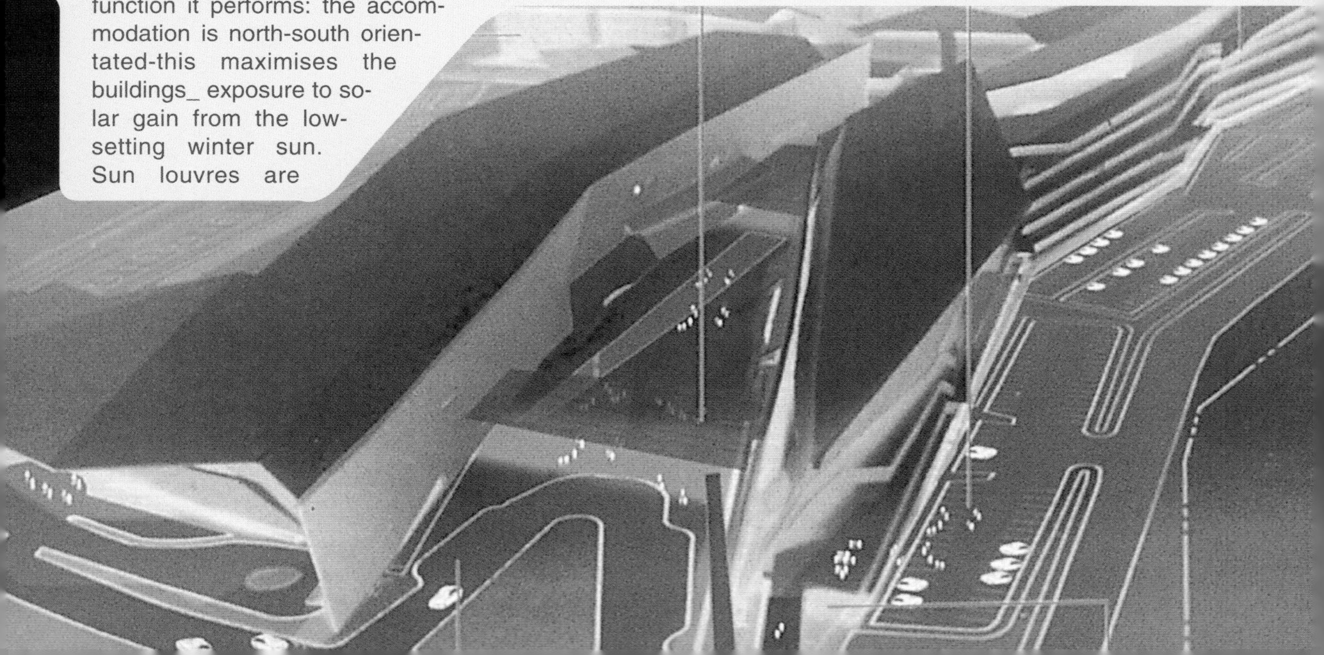

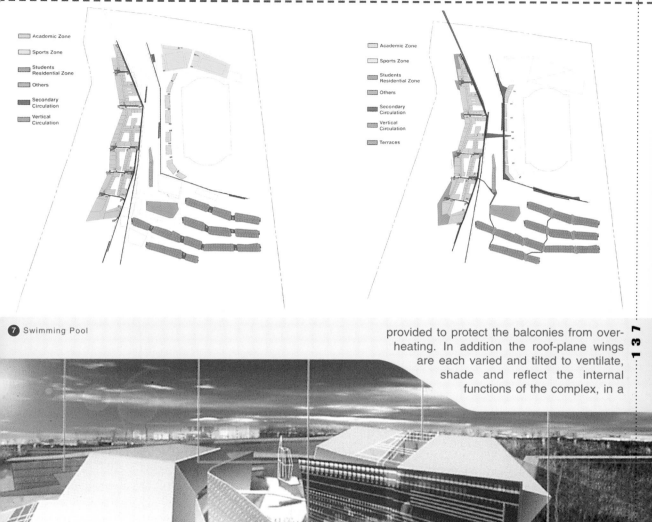

Academic Zone
Sports Zone
Students Residential Zone
Others
Secondary Circulation
Vertical Circulation

Academic Zone
Sports Zone
Students Residential Zone
Others
Secondary Circulation
Vertical Circulation
Terraces

7 Swimming Pool

provided to protect the balconies from overheating. In addition the roof-plane wings are each varied and tilted to ventilate, shade and reflect the internal functions of the complex, in a

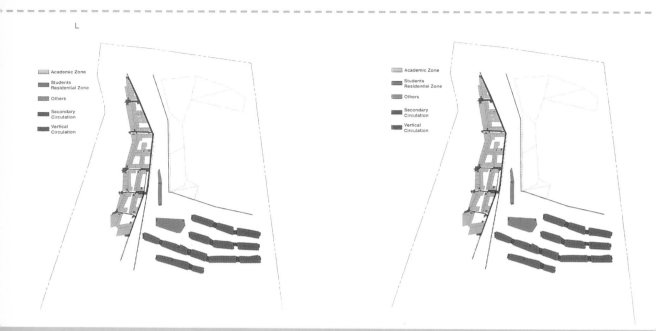

The project, in its essence, is a massive bioclimatic canopy spreading as an array of wings, distributed alongside the fuselage of the inclined spinal planes of the pedestrian concourse. The central ideas of the project are as much about the section, as they are the masterplan: the fundamental framework of a Sunpath Groundscraper.

The Green Spine

sime darby
& condomi

2.1 2.2 2.3 2.4 2.5 2.6 2.7 2.8 2.9 2.10 2.11 2.12 2

Cotton Stainers

"Libelle"

ranging from 2-6storeys no.ofstoreys 23.42acres SiteArea   nett: 699 200sq.ft.(offices) 400 00sq.ft.(condominium)gross: 874 000sq.ft.(c

headquarters
niums : KL

4 2.15 2.16 2.17 2.18 2.19 2.20 2.21 2.22 2.23 2.24 2.25

3.1 3.2 3.3 credits

"Gottesanbeterin"
Bulls-Eye Mantodea

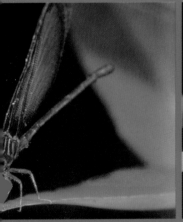

633 331sq.ft.(condominium) Area Sime Darby Client   Kuala Lumpur Golf & Country Club, Kuala Lumpur, Malaysia Location ▬ Project Data ▬

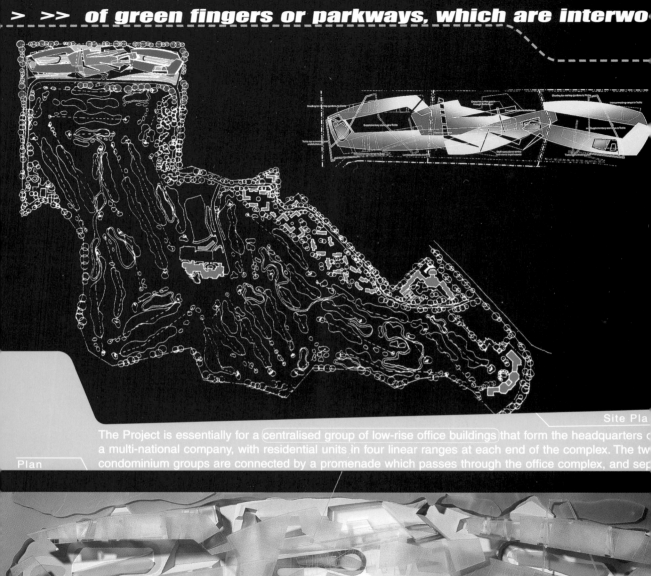

The Project is essentially for a centralised group of low-rise office buildings that form the headquarters o
a multi-national company, with residential units in four linear ranges at each end of the complex. The tw

Plan

condominium groups are connected by a promenade which passes through the office complex, and sep

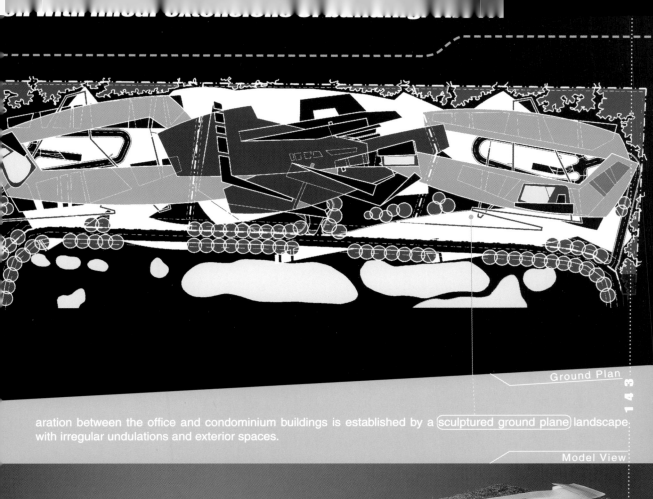

Ground Plan

aration between the office and condominium buildings is established by a (sculptured ground plane) landscape with irregular undulations and exterior spaces.

Model View

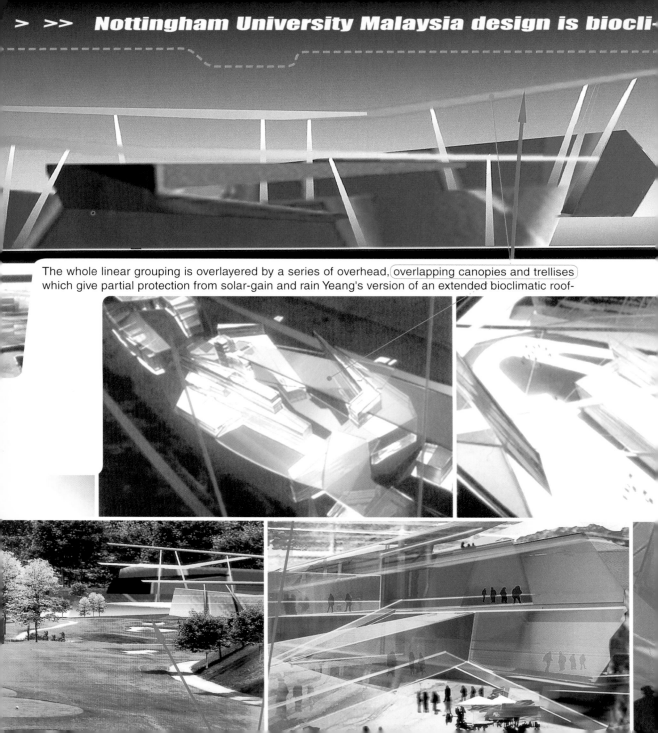

The whole linear grouping is overlayered by a series of overhead, overlapping canopies and trellises which give partial protection from solar-gain and rain Yeang's version of an extended bioclimatic roof-

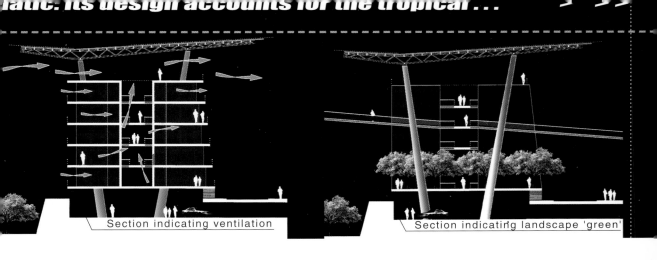

Section indicating ventilation

Section indicating landscape 'green'

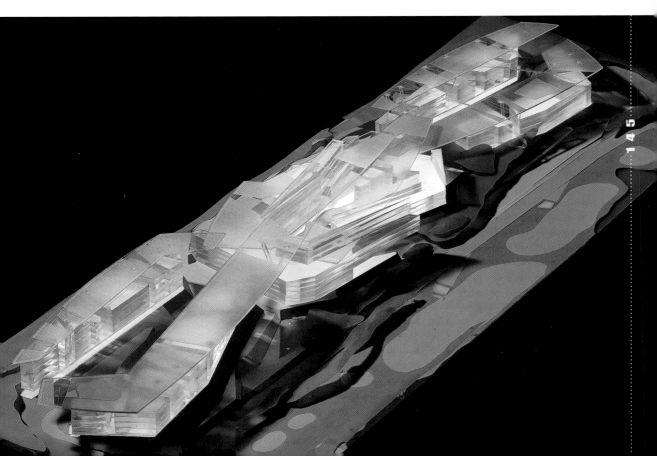

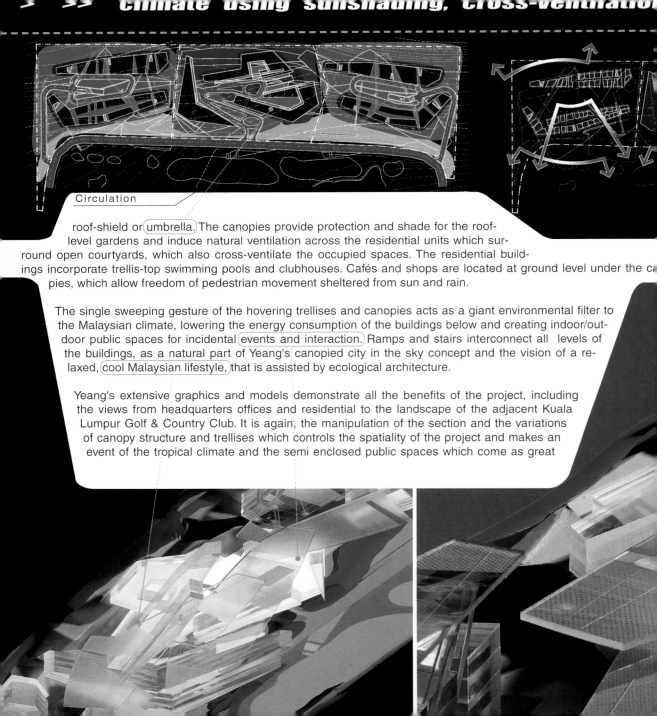

Circulation

roof-shield or umbrella. The canopies provide protection and shade for the roof-level gardens and induce natural ventilation across the residential units which surround open courtyards, which also cross-ventilate the occupied spaces. The residential buildings incorporate trellis-top swimming pools and clubhouses. Cafés and shops are located at ground level under the canopies, which allow freedom of pedestrian movement sheltered from sun and rain.

The single sweeping gesture of the hovering trellises and canopies acts as a giant environmental filter to the Malaysian climate, lowering the energy consumption of the buildings below and creating indoor/outdoor public spaces for incidental events and interaction. Ramps and stairs interconnect all levels of the buildings, as a natural part of Yeang's canopied city in the sky concept and the vision of a relaxed, cool Malaysian lifestyle, that is assisted by ecological architecture.

Yeang's extensive graphics and models demonstrate all the benefits of the project, including the views from headquarters offices and residential to the landscape of the adjacent Kuala Lumpur Golf & Country Club. It is again, the manipulation of the section and the variations of canopy structure and trellises which controls the spatiality of the project and makes an event of the tropical climate and the semi enclosed public spaces which come as great

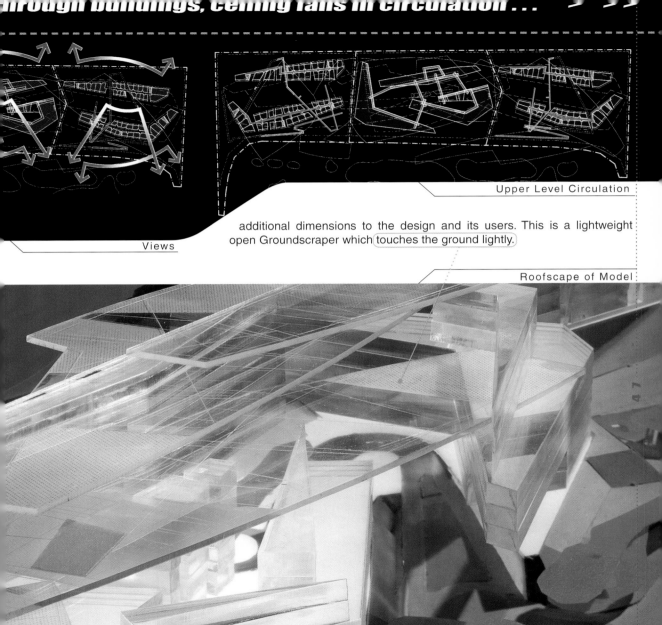

Upper Level Circulation

Views

additional dimensions to the design and its users. This is a lightweight open Groundscraper which touches the ground lightly.

Roofscape of Model

marsham
urban

11storeys no.ofstoreys 20 000sq.m. SiteArea   residential: 16 000sq.m. commercial: 5 500sq.m. total lettable: 85 000sq.m. total open s

2.14 2.15 **2.16** 2.17 2.18 2.19 2.20 2.21 2.22 2.23 2.24 2.25

3.1 3.2 3.3 credits

street design

— Project Data —

15 500 sq.m. office: 56 000 sq.m retail/leisure: 8 500 sq.m. Areas   D.O.E. Client 53°N Latitude   Marsham Street/Horseferry Road, London Location

	A		B		C		D		E		F	
level 9												
level 8 B												
level 8												
level 7												
level 6												
level 5												
level 4												
level 3												
level 2												
level 1												
level G												
level B 1												
level B 2												

Legend
- office space
- residential
- office
- retail

1. Internal gallery
2. Ramps and travelator
3. Residential
4. Office (private sector)
5. Retail shopping unit
6. Vertical circulation infrastructure

Yeang's approach to his first major London proposal takes the form of what he describes as an Urban Design in a three-dimensional matrix of land uses and occupancy. These uses include Retail, Private & Public Offices

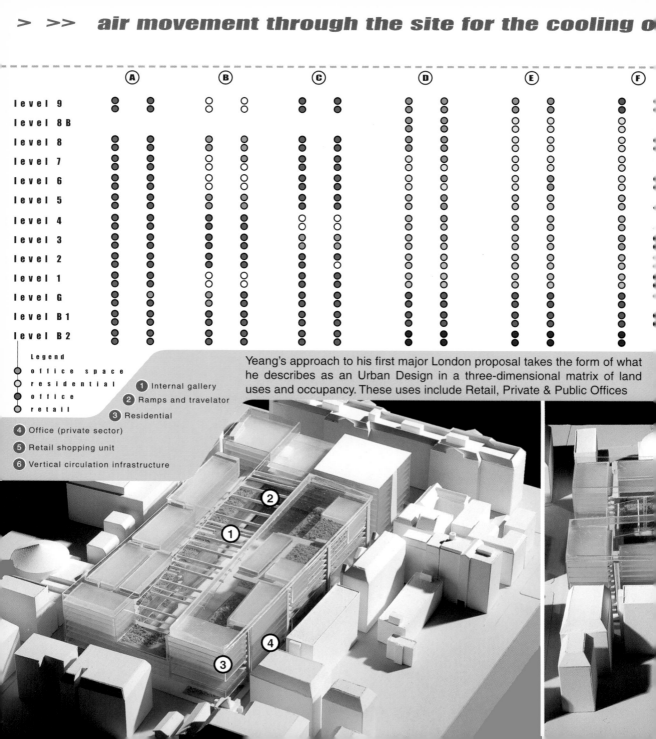

Ⓖ   Ⓗ   Ⓙ   Ⓚ   Ⓛ   Ⓜ

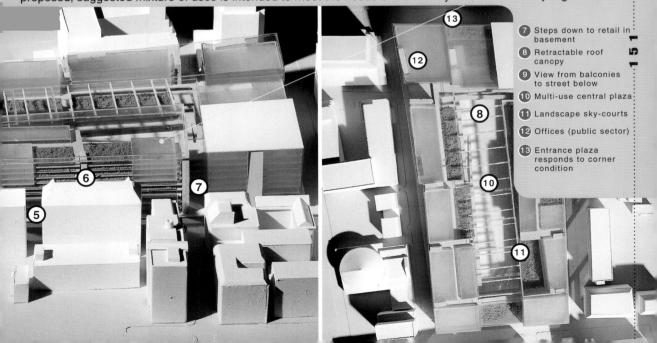

Offices together with residential, leisure and restaurants and associated parking areas for office and residential use. The occupancy of space is arranged by level and by plan and section area, in a colour-coded diagram. The proposed, suggested mixture of uses is intended to meet the needs of the locality and its necessary regeneration.

7 Steps down to retail in basement

8 Retractable roof canopy

9 View from balconies to street below

10 Multi-use central plaza

11 Landscape sky-courts

12 Offices (public sector)

13 Entrance plaza responds to corner condition

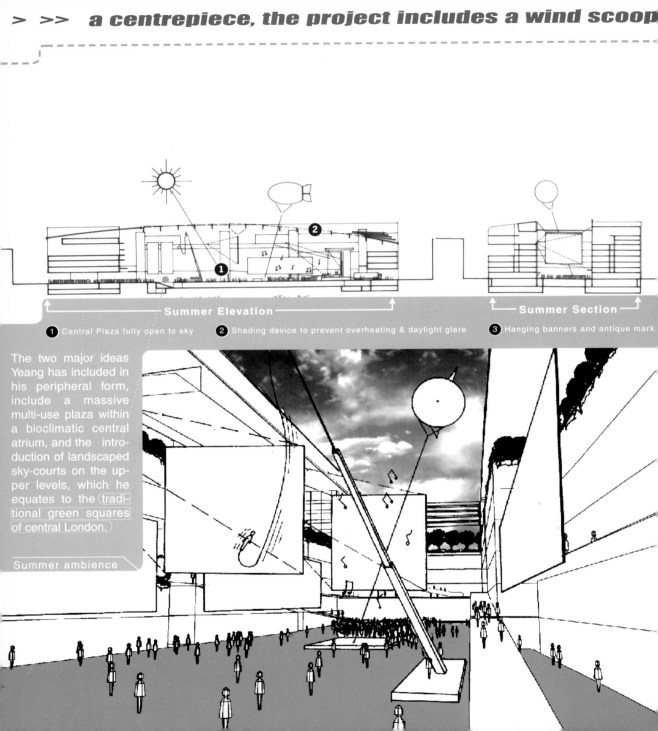

Summer Elevation

Summer Section

1 Central Plaza fully open to sky **2** Shading device to prevent overheating & daylight glare **3** Hanging banners and antique mark

The two major ideas Yeang has included in his peripheral form, include a massive multi-use plaza within a bioclimatic central atrium, and the introduction of landscaped sky-courts on the upper levels, which he equates to the traditional green squares of central London.

Summer ambience

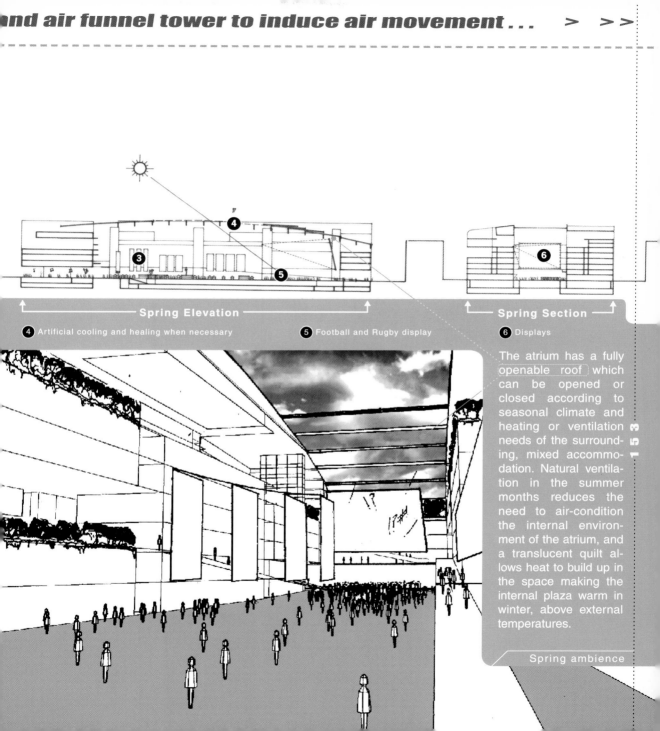

Spring Elevation

Spring Section

④ Artificial cooling and heating when necessary

⑤ Football and Rugby display

⑥ Displays

The atrium has a fully openable roof which can be opened or closed according to seasonal climate and heating or ventilation needs of the surrounding, mixed accommodation. Natural ventilation in the summer months reduces the need to air-condition the internal environment of the atrium, and a translucent quilt allows heat to build up in the space making the internal plaza warm in winter, above external temperatures.

Spring ambience

153

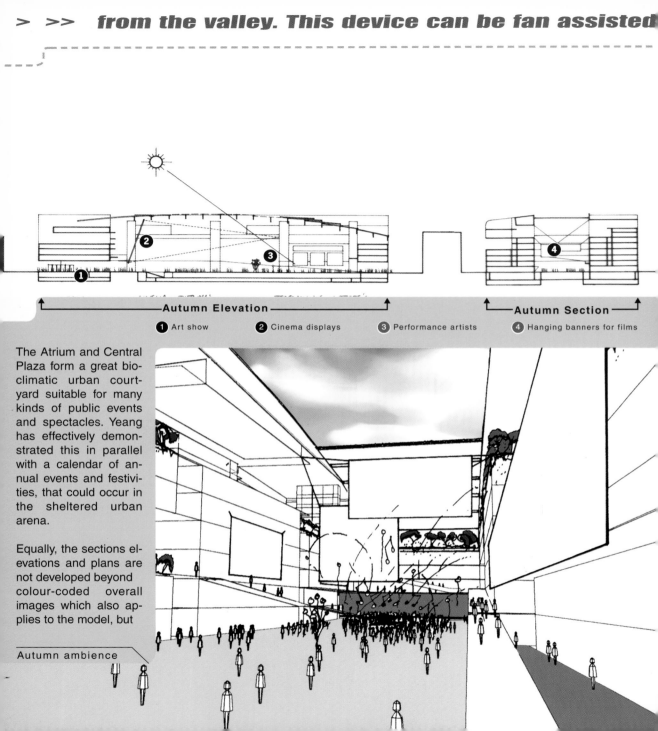

Autumn Elevation

Autumn Section

1 Art show   2 Cinema displays   3 Performance artists   4 Hanging banners for films

The Atrium and Central Plaza form a great bio-climatic urban court-yard suitable for many kinds of public events and spectacles. Yeang has effectively demon-strated this in parallel with a calendar of an-nual events and festivi-ties, that could occur in the sheltered urban arena.

Equally, the sections el-evations and plans are not developed beyond colour-coded overall images which also ap-plies to the model, but

Autumn ambience

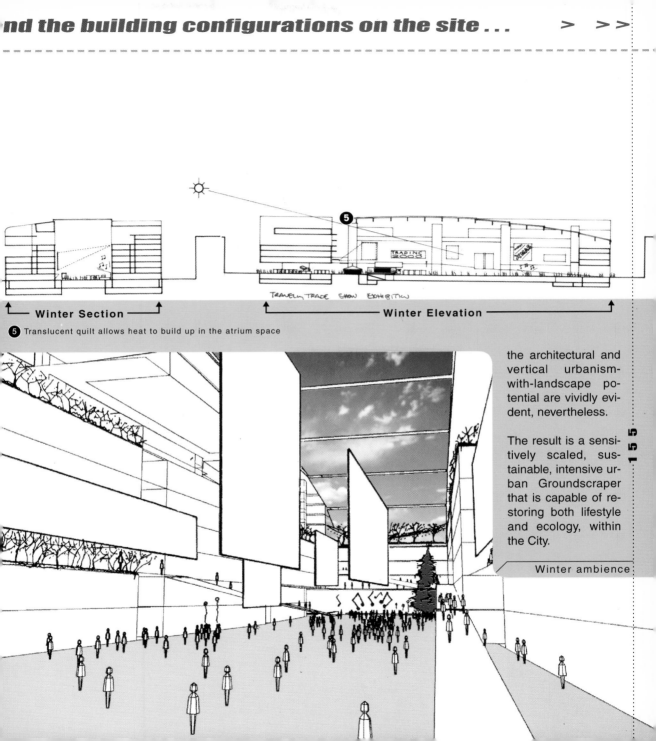

Winter Section

Winter Elevation

TRAVELLING TRADE SHOW EXHIBITION

⑤ Translucent quilt allows heat to build up in the atrium space

the architectural and vertical urbanism-with-landscape potential are vividly evident, nevertheless.

The result is a sensitively scaled, sustainable, intensive urban Groundscraper that is capable of restoring both lifestyle and ecology, within the City.

Winter ambience

155

capital plaza

2.1   2.2   2.3 2.4   2.5 2.6 2.7 2.8 2.9 2.10 2.11 2.12 2

Planning Area: 323 350sq.m Design Area: 235 630sq.m SiteArea   Carparking provision: 627 cps Basement Carparking Area: 21 86

: taipei

2.14 2.15 2.16 2.17 2.18 2.19 2.20 2.21 2.22 2.23 2.24 2.25

3.13.2 3.3 credits

osed Area: 14 927sq.m Areas Bureau of Urban Development, Taipei City GovernmentClient 25°NLatitude Taipei, Taiwan Location — Project Data —

25°00'N 121°40'E

Dec — Jan — Feb — Winter   March — April — May — Spring   June — July — Aug — Summer   Sept — Oct — Nov — Autumn

Wind

Humidity (%)
Temperature (°C)
Precipitation (mm)

1400 hours
0600 hours
maximum
minimum

jan · feb · mar · apr · may · jun · jul · aug · sept · oct · nov · dec

Presidential Office

Chong Qing South Road
Presidential Plaza
Light Beacon
Huai Ning Street
Taipei Museum
Continuous Green
Glass Plaza & Performance stage
228 Memorial
Cultural Plaza

Chung Shan Street
Underground Passage
Taipei Guest Hall
Beacon Boulevard

— **Section BB** —

At first sight, there is a striking similiarity in terms of urban hierarchy between the East-to-West Plaza axis in Taipei and the great western axis of Paris, which links the Palais du Louvre, via the Place de la Concorde _ Champs Elysées and Arc de Triomphe to the modern commercial center of La Défense with its recent Grande Arche installation.

1 Presidential Plaza
2 Glass Plaza
3 Continuous Green to 288 Memorial
4 East-West Axial Boulevard

Double Ten Military Parade

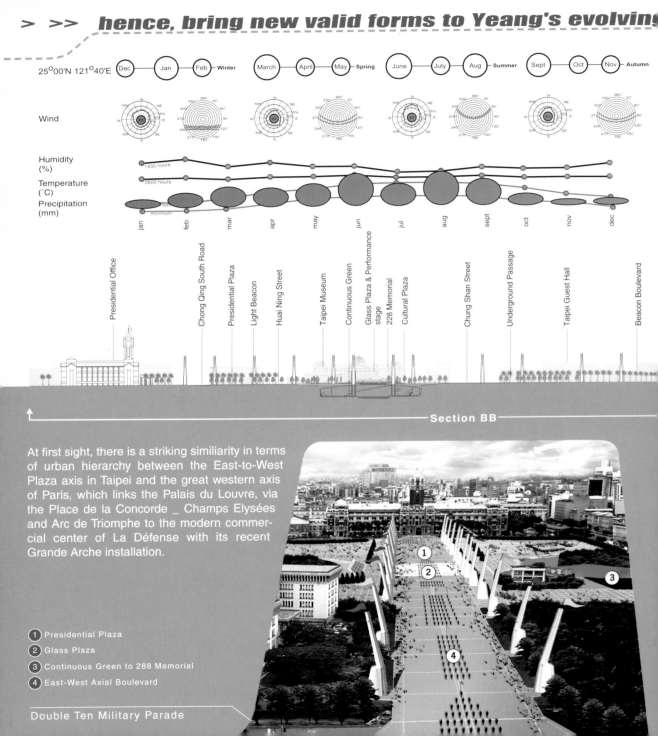

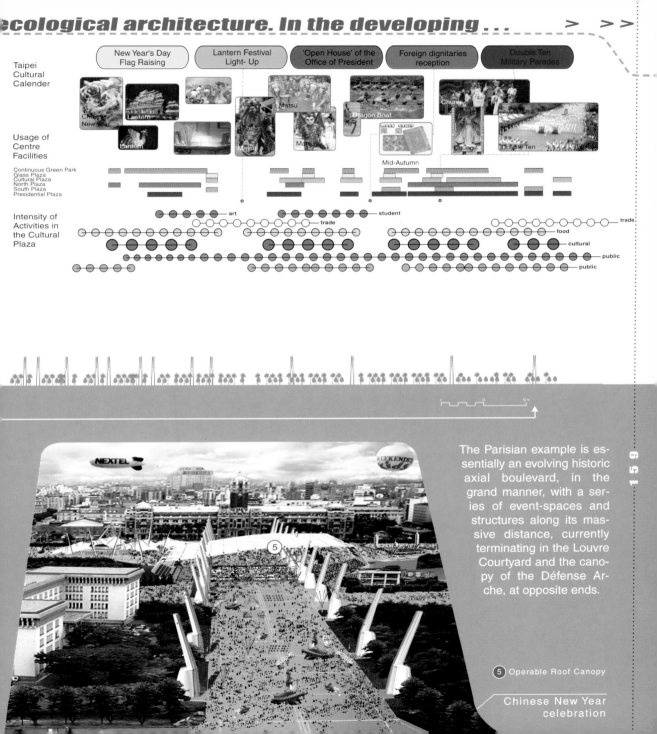

Taipei Cultural Calender

| New Year's Day Flag Raising | Lantern Festival Light- Up | 'Open House' of the Office of President | Foreign dignitaries reception | Double Ten Military Parades |

Chinese New Year
Lantern
Qing
Lantern
Qing
Matsu
Matsu
Matsu
Dragon Boat
Mid-Autumn
Chung
Chung
Double Ten

Usage of Centre Facilities

Continuous Green Park
Glass Plaza
Cultural Plaza
North Plaza
South Plaza
Presidential Plaza

Intensity of Activities in the Cultural Plaza

art
student
trade
trade
food
cultural
public
public

The Parisian example is essentially an evolving historic axial boulevard, in the grand manner, with a series of event-spaces and structures along its massive distance, currently terminating in the Louvre Courtyard and the canopy of the Défense Arche, at opposite ends.

NEXTEL
WEEKENDER

(5) Operable Roof Canopy

Chinese New Year celebration

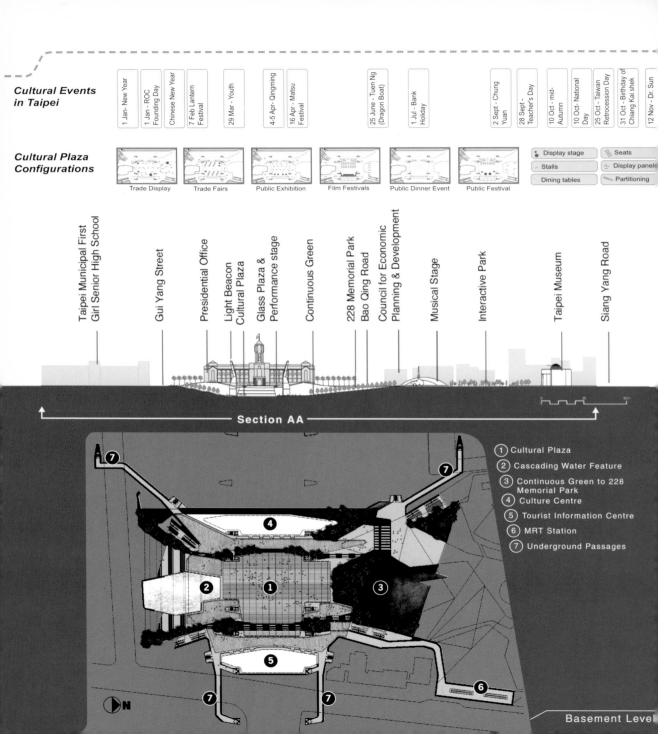

Cultural Events in Taipei

- 1 Jan- New Year
- 1 Jan - ROC Founding Day
- Chinese New Year
- 7 Feb Lantern Festival
- 29 Mar - Youth
- 4-5 Apr- Qingming
- 16 Apr- Matsu Festival
- 25 June - Tuen Ng (Dragon Boat)
- 1 Jul - Bank Holiday
- 2 Sept - Chung Yuan
- 28 Sept - Teacher's Day
- 10 Oct- mid-Autumn
- 10 Oct- National Day
- 25 Oct - Taiwan Retrocession Day
- 31 Oct - Birthday of Chiang Kai shek
- 12 Nov - Dr. Sun

Cultural Plaza Configurations

Trade Display | Trade Fairs | Public Exhibition | Film Festivals | Public Dinner Event | Public Festival

- Display stage
- Stalls
- Dining tables
- Seats
- Display panels
- Partitioning

Taipei Municipal First Girl Senior High School

Gui Yang Street

Presidential Office

Light Beacon Cultural Plaza

Glass Plaza & Performance stage

Continuous Green

228 Memorial Park Bao Qing Road

Council for Economic Planning & Development

Musical Stage

Interactive Park

Taipei Museum

Siang Yang Road

Section AA

1. Cultural Plaza
2. Cascading Water Feature
3. Continuous Green to 228 Memorial Park
4. Culture Centre
5. Tourist Information Centre
6. MRT Station
7. Underground Passages

N

Basement Level

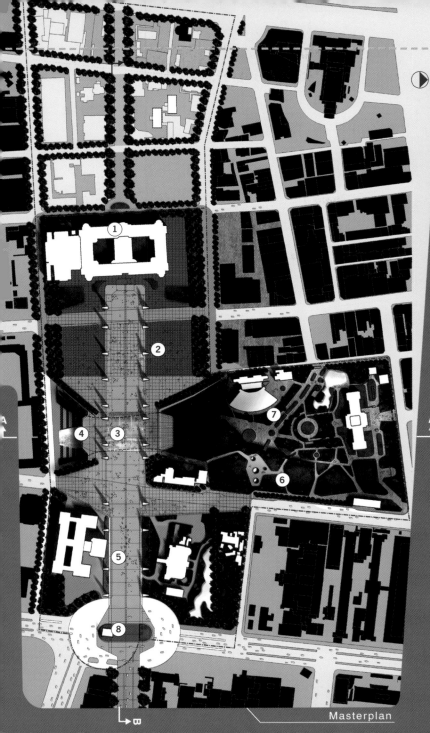

The Taipei project has given Yeang the opportunity, at once, to design a Cultural Project in the grand manner, and on a scale he has not previously encountered but on rare occasions. His solution is largely centred on The Glass Plaza _ a public space and structure hovering within and submerged below the main Boulevard level. The Capital Plaza project is appropriately addressed to the entire 5 kilometre axial strip or Boulevard, stretching from the Office of the President in the west to the City Hall in the east _ the two poles of political centre and city-administration.

A

1 Office of the President
2 Presidential Plaza
3 Glass Plaza
4 Raised Seating Area
5 East-West Axial Boulevard
6 Interactive Park
7 Museum Park
8 East Gate

Masterplan

The axial strip between the Presidential Office and City Hall is emphasized by a series of super-bright-lights, to be turned on during festivals and other significant occasions, together with a massive landscape and hardscape programme. The lighting pylons are joined by 12 monumental pairs of centennial columns, which are also illuminated at night, defining the Presidential office plaza.

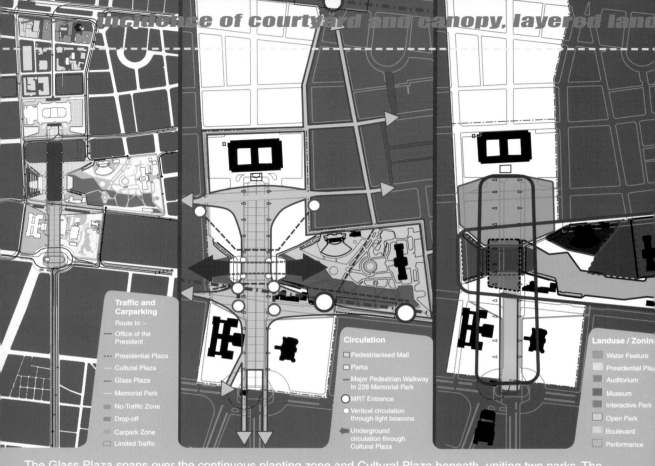

Traffic and Carparking
Route to :-
— Office of the President
--- Presidential Plaza
— Cultural Plaza
— Glass Plaza
— Memorial Park
No-Traffic Zone
Drop-off
Carpark Zone
Limited Traffic

Circulation
☐ Pedestrianised Mall
☐ Parks
--- Major Pedestrian Walkway in 228 Memorial Park
◯ MRT Entrance
◯ Vertical circulation through light beacons
➤ Underground circulation through Cultural Plaza

Landuse / Zonin...
Water Feature
Presidential Plaz...
Auditorium
Museum
Interactive Park
Open Park
Boulevard
Performance

The Glass Plaza spans over the continuous planting zone and Cultural Plaza beneath, uniting two parks. The Glass Plaza floor provides natural daylighting to the sunken Cultural Plaza, and is transformed into a glowing

Glass Plaza

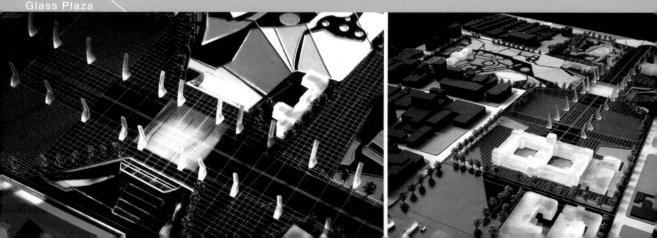

°00'N 121°40'E

Winter	Spring	Summer	Autumn
Dec Jan Feb	March April May	June July Aug	Sept Oct Nov

Glass Roof over Cultural Plaza for solar warming

Variable air exhaust depending on external conditions

Operable roof over Glass Plaza

Variable air exhaust depending on external conditions

Plan

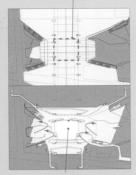 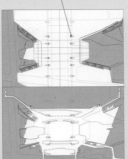 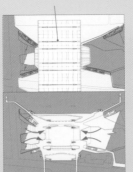 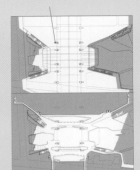

Operable Screens are shut in winter to retain heat in the cultural plaza

Blowers utilising the water feature as a cooling element cirulates cool air into the cultural plaza

Penetration of light through Glass Plaza

Operable roof over Glass Plaza provides shade to stage area

Section

Glass roof over Cultural Plaza for solar warming and Operable Screens are shut to retain heat

Cross

Blowers utilising the water feature as a cooling element cirulates cool air into the Cultural Glass Plaza

horizontal beacon at night. The Glass Plaza also serves as an outdoor performance area with raised seating areas on the north and south sides. The space, or Arena, can also be covered with a mechanically operable

Continuous Green to 228 Memorial Park

Axial Boulevard

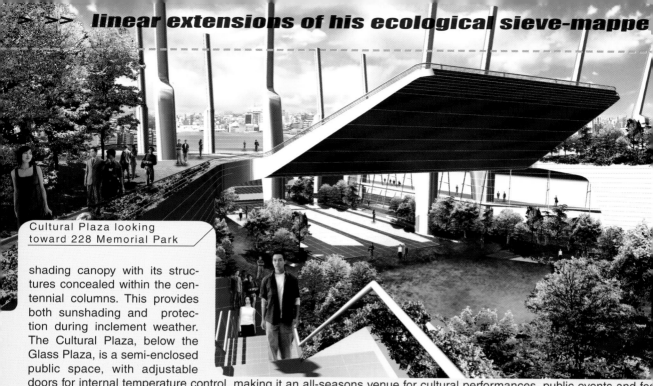

Cultural Plaza looking toward 228 Memorial Park

shading canopy with its structures concealed within the centennial columns. This provides both sunshading and protection during inclement weather. The Cultural Plaza, below the Glass Plaza, is a semi-enclosed public space, with adjustable doors for internal temperature control, making it an all-seasons venue for cultural performances, public events and festive celebrations. Other devices generally control the public space environment including shading, ventilation and wind flow for cooling.

The Capital Plaza design i organised by feng shui (geomancy) principles, uniting with the roots of the origina Taipei city. The historic natur of the precinct is also define by a series of light beacon along the boundary of the ol city walls, as a visual memor of the city's origin.

The project, as a whole, is a massive Cultural Ground scraper based on ecologica principles its counterpart i found in the Taipei Er Me subscraper, in the occupatio of the linear public realm.

Cultural Plaza

Cultural Plaza

bishopsgate

approx.3.4 hectares

Site Area   gross:157 000sq.m.net:117 000sq.m. plantation: 770 000sq.m.& circulation Areas   The Architecture Foundation (in association with), Peabody Tr

2.14 2.15 2.16 2.17 2.18 2.19 2.20 2.21 2.22 2.23 2.24 2.25

3.13.2 3.3 credits

masterplan:
london

British Steel (Sponsor) Client   Bishopsgate Goodsyard, London Boroughs of Hackney & Tower Hamlets, London E1 Location —Project Data —

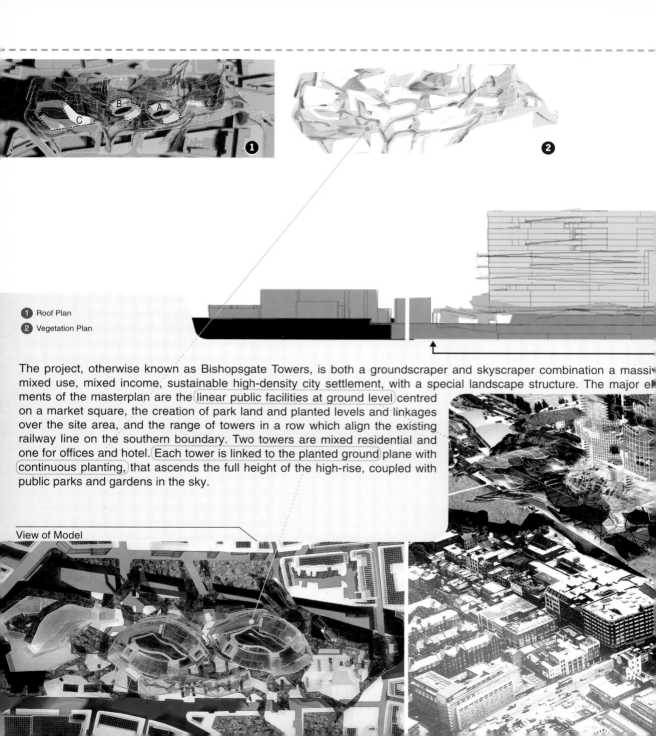

① Roof Plan
② Vegetation Plan

The project, otherwise known as Bishopsgate Towers, is both a groundscraper and skyscraper combination a massiv mixed use, mixed income, sustainable high-density city settlement, with a special landscape structure. The major el ments of the masterplan are the linear public facilities at ground level centred on a market square, the creation of park land and planted levels and linkages over the site area, and the range of towers in a row which align the existing railway line on the southern boundary. Two towers are mixed residential and one for offices and hotel. Each tower is linked to the planted ground plane with continuous planting, that ascends the full height of the high-rise, coupled with public parks and gardens in the sky.

View of Model

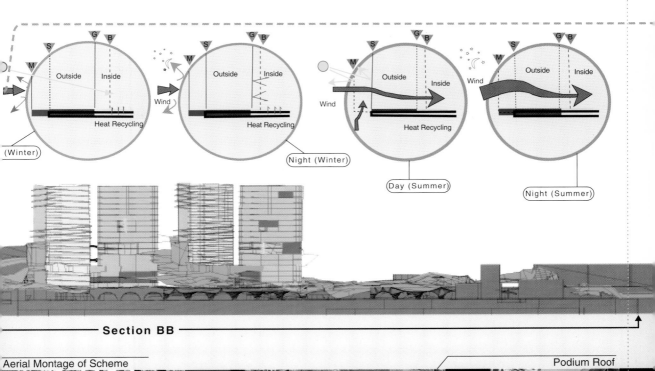

Outside | Inside
Heat Recycling
(Winter)

Outside | Inside
Wind
Heat Recycling
Night (Winter)

Outside | Inside
Wind
Heat Recycling
Day (Summer)

Outside | Inside
Wind
Night (Summer)

Section BB

Aerial Montage of Scheme

Podium Roof

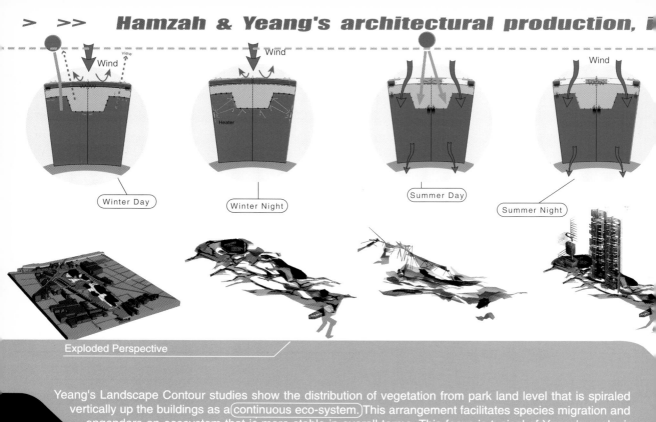

Winter Day

Wind

view

Winter Night

Heater

Summer Day

Wind

Wind

Summer Night

Exploded Perspective

Yeang's Landscape Contour studies show the distribution of vegetation from park land level that is spiraled vertically up the buildings as a continuous eco-system. This arrangement facilitates species migration and engenders an ecosystem that is more stable in overall terms. This focus is typical of Yeang's ecological architecture and its whole agenda, which is applied to this design, and in particular the sustainable aspects of building large developments. For the first time in Europe, Yeang then rehearses his complete ecological design system, including the partitioned matrix which incorporates interdependencies, systems and environment, and allows the assessment of the environ-

Sectional View of Model

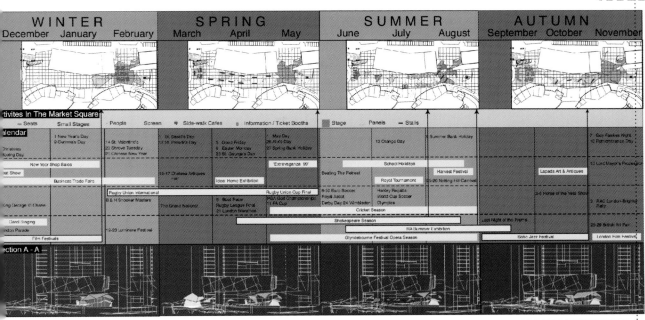

	WINTER			SPRING			SUMMER			AUTUMN		
	December	January	February	March	April	May	June	July	August	September	October	November

Activities In The Market Square
— Seats   Small Stages   · People   Screen   Side-walk Cafes   Information / Ticket Booths   Stage   Panels   — Stalls

Calendar

		1 New Year's Day	14 St. Valentine's	St. David's Day	5 Good Friday	May Day		13 Orange Day	Summer Bank Holiday			7 Guy Fawkes Night
		9 Gemma's Day	20 Shrove Tuesday	17,18 Patrick's Day	6 Easter Monday	26 Ali's Day						10 Remembrance Day
	Christmas		20 Chinese New Year			27 Spring Bank Holiday						
	Boxing Day				23 St. George's Day							
		New Year Shop Sales				'Extravaganza '97'		School Holidays			13 Lord Mayor's Procession	
	Toy Show						Beating The Retreat		Harvest Festival			
		Business Trade Fairs	15-17 Chelsea Antiques Fair		Ideal Home Exhibition			Royal Tournament	25-30 Notting Hill Carnival	Lapada Art & Antiques		
	King George VI Chase	Rugby Union International			6 Boat Race	Rugby Union Cup Final	8-30 Euro Soccer	Henley Regatta				
		B & H Snooker Masters			Rugby League Final	PGA Golf Championship	Royal Ascot	World Cup Soccer		3-6 Horse of the Year Show		3 RAC London-Brighton Rally
	David Singing	The Grand National		21 London Marathon	11 FA Cup	Derby Day 24 Wimbledon	Olympics				
						Cricket Season					
	London Parade				Shakespeare Season			Last Night of the Proms		23-29 British Art Fair	
		19-23 Luminere Festival				RA Summer Exhibition					
	Film Festivals			Glyndebourne Festival Opera Season						Soho Jazz Festival	London Film Festival

Section A - A

(Seasonal Mapping of Cultural Activities within the Market Square)

mental consequences of the built system. Fundamental to this assessment is the study of the existing site's ecosystem, which Yeang concludes is a totally urbanised 'zero culture' site. Hence the major design strategy is to increase its

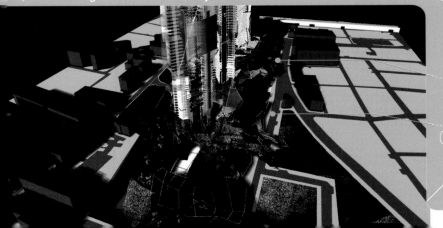

organic mass by revegetating the site in order to rehabilitate the site's ecosystem the result is the Parks and the vertical landscaping the basis of the groundscraper is therefore structures embedded in its (landscape element) a central park at levels 2 & 3 located above street level and accessible by (landscaped ramps.)

(Increase of Organic Mass at Podium Level)

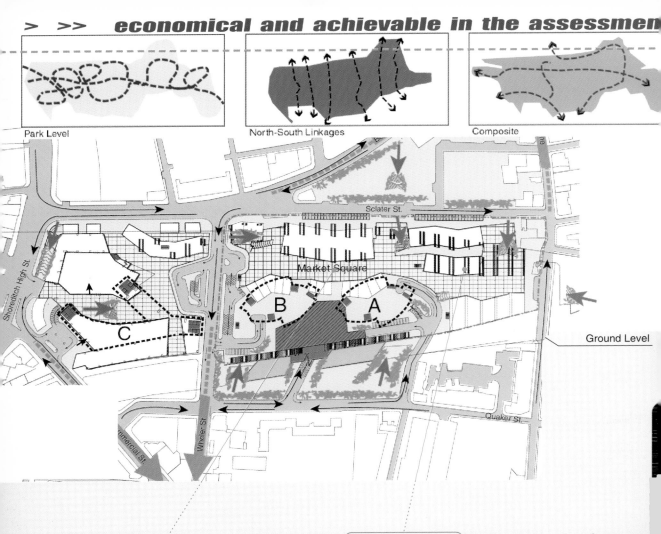

Park Level

North-South Linkages

Composite

Ground Level

The public programme at ground level, partially contained in existing brick-arches, includes retail, art & craft centre, studios and workshops and gallery with adjacent features such as greenhouse & an aviary. The linear arrangement surrounds a market square, which is designed for usage throughout the year.

The towers are essentially of Yeang's green skyscraper series, with residential content of apartments and houses providing a socially sustainable mix. The various designs incorporate gardens (front and back), with movable shutters for weather protection. The towers incorporate ramp access and include many of Yeang's bioclimatic elements such as the service cores as a shield.

Bishopsgate is the first example, in London, of Yeang's ecological design applied at maximum resolution to an urban village a sustainable settlement of high-density.

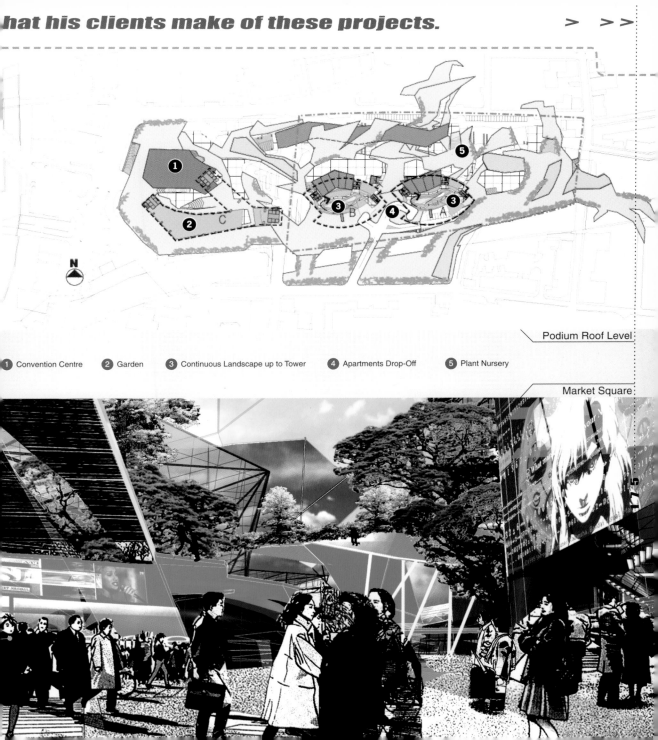

Podium Roof Level

① Convention Centre   ② Garden   ③ Continuous Landscape up to Tower   ④ Apartments Drop-Off   ⑤ Plant Nursery

Market Square

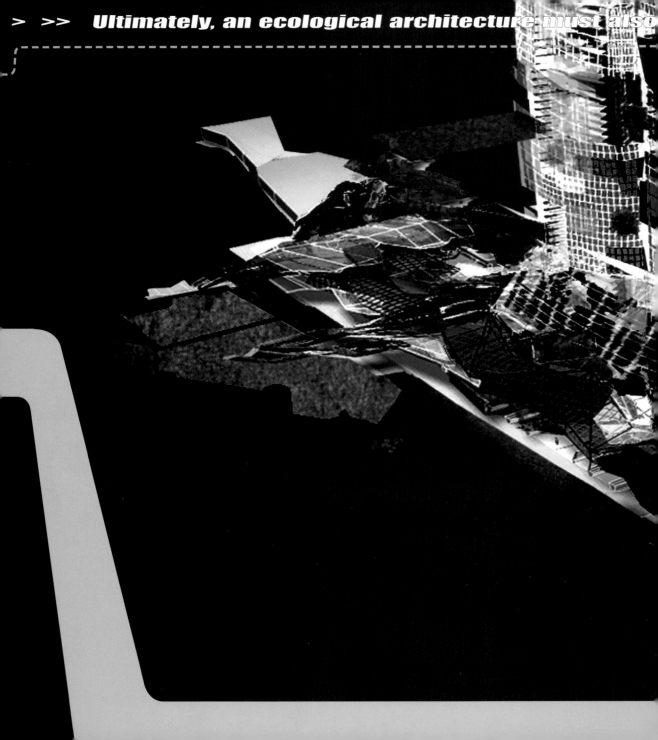

> >> *its own integral aesthetic systems. That this is th*

2.1 2.2 2.3 2.4 2.5 2.6 2.7 2.8 2.9 2.10 2.11 2.12 2.

content page 1.1 1.2 1.3

al-asima village:

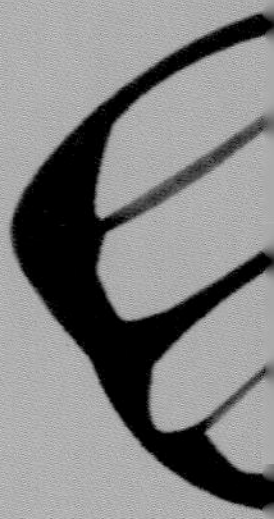

Handmaidens - 'Lepidoptera'

Narrow Forewings + Small Hindwings

gross (excluding carparking): 140 460sq.m net : 102,00sq.m carparking provision: 2 000 carparking spaces Areas 3-storey podium shopping block 4-storey independant offic

4 |2 . 15 |2 . 16 |2 . 17 |2 . 18 |**2 . 19** |2 . 20 | 2 . 21 | 2 . 2 |22 . 23 |2 . 24 |2 . 2 5

3 . 13 . 23 . 3 c r e d i t s

shopping
kuwait

40 Storey Signature Office Tower no.ofstoreys Salhia Real Estate Company K.S.CClient 29.4°N Latitude Kuwait Location ▬**Project Data** ▬

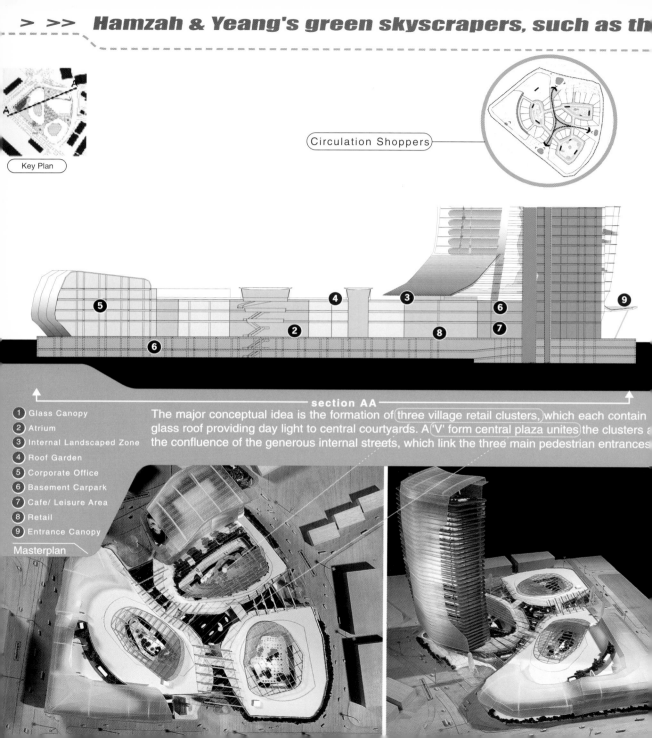

Key Plan

Circulation Shoppers

⑤ ② ④ ③ ⑥ ⑨
⑥ ⑧ ⑦

—— section AA ——

The major conceptual idea is the formation of three village retail clusters, which each contain glass roof providing day light to central courtyards. A 'V' form central plaza unites the clusters a the confluence of the generous internal streets, which link the three main pedestrian entrances

① Glass Canopy
② Atrium
③ Internal Landscaped Zone
④ Roof Garden
⑤ Corporate Office
⑥ Basement Carpark
⑦ Cafe/ Leisure Area
⑧ Retail
⑨ Entrance Canopy

Masterplan

DITT Tower for Singapore, of 1998.

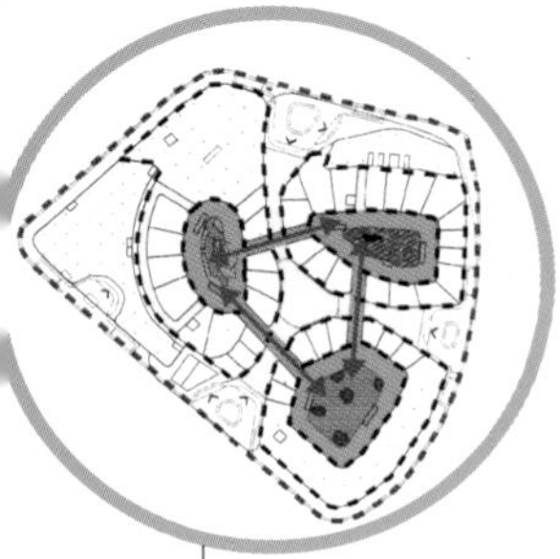

Retail Concept

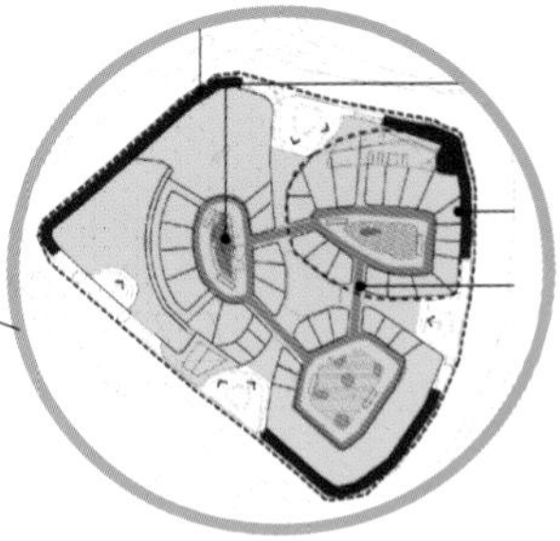

Planting Concept

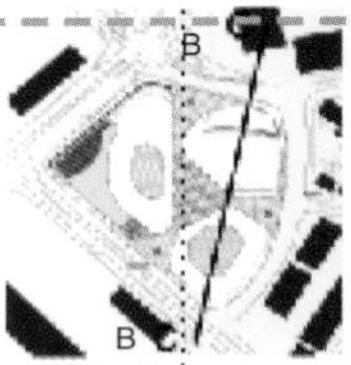

Key Plan

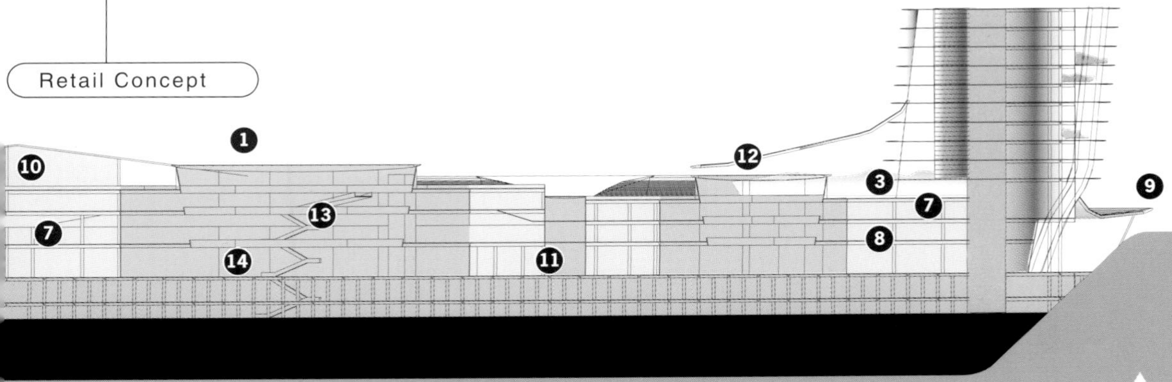

section CC

Evaporative cooling towers are positioned at roof-level of these entrances, which provide natural coolth for the users before they enter the air-conditioned environment of the organic malls and retail spaces. The towers also provide an important urban-symbol for the whole complex and a signal of the points of entry.

(10) Cinema Complex
(11) Internal Street
(12) Glass Canopy Skylight
(13) Ramp to Podium Level
(14) International Cuisine Hall

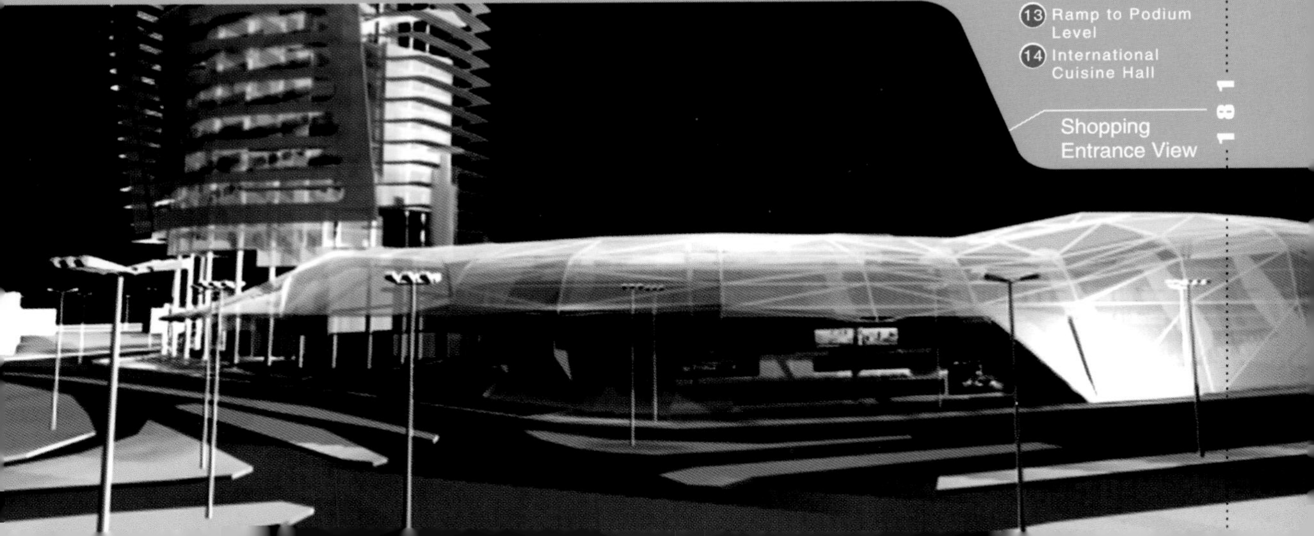

Shopping Entrance View

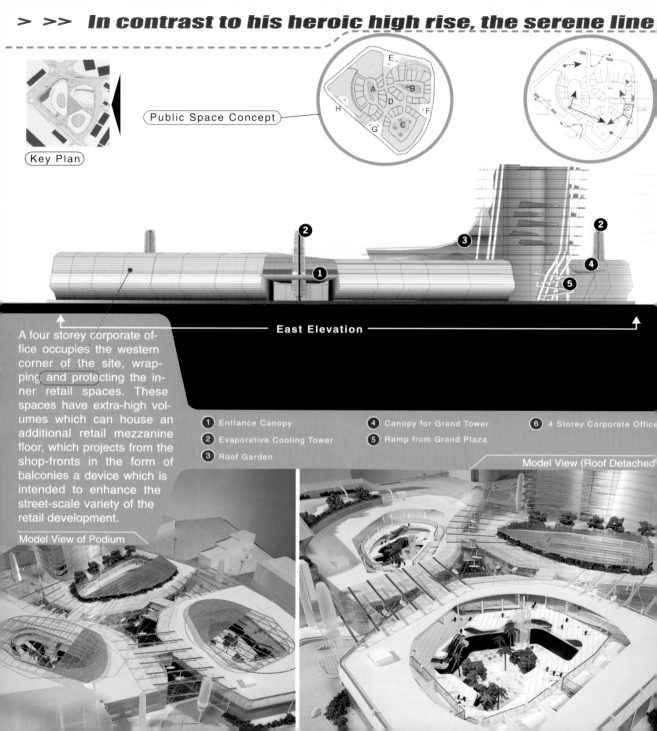

Key Plan

Public Space Concept

East Elevation

A four storey corporate office occupies the western corner of the site, wrapping and protecting the inner retail spaces. These spaces have extra-high volumes which can house an additional retail mezzanine floor, which projects from the shop-fronts in the form of balconies a device which is intended to enhance the street-scale variety of the retail development.

Model View of Podium

1. Entrance Canopy
2. Evaporative Cooling Tower
3. Roof Garden
4. Canopy for Grand Tower
5. Ramp from Grand Plaza
6. 4 Storey Corporate Office

Model View (Roof Detached)

Circulation : Vehicular

Landuse

Key Plan

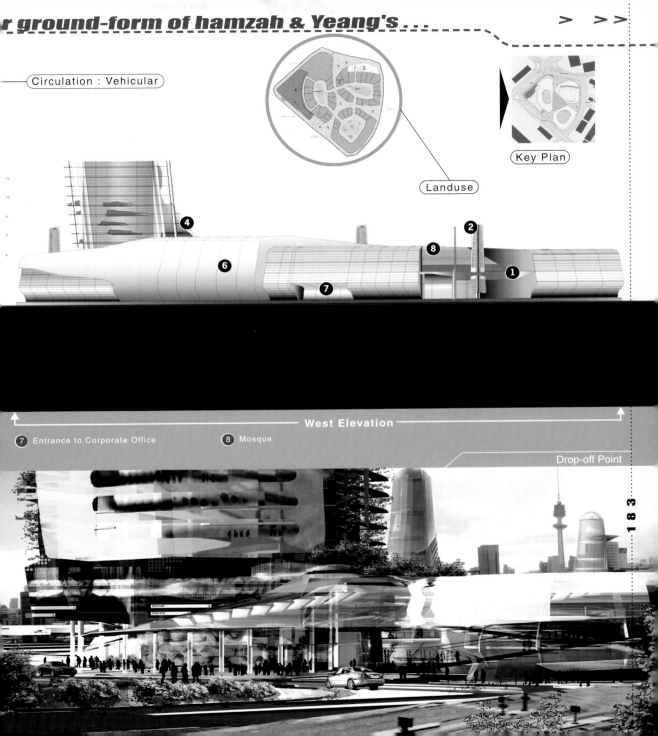

West Elevation

⑦ Entrance to Corporate Office   ⑧ Mosque

Drop-off Point

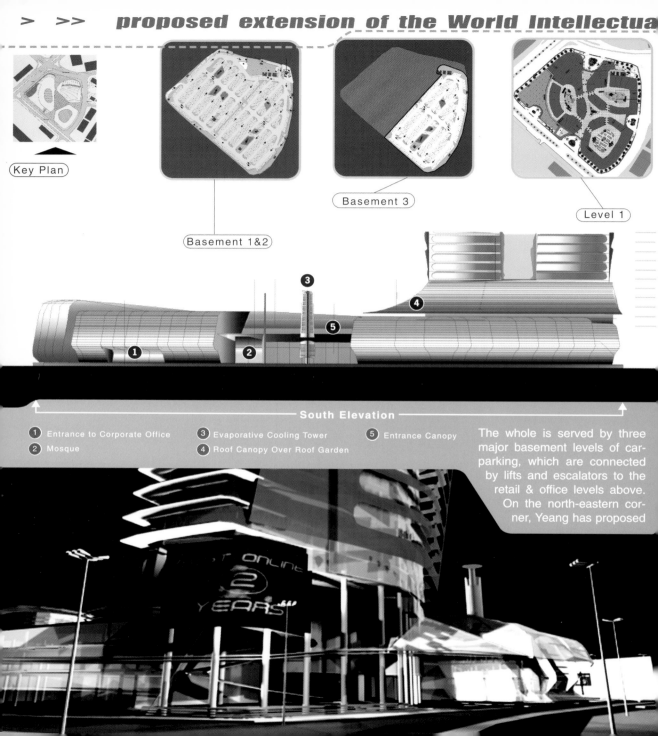

Key Plan

Basement 1&2

Basement 3

Level 1

South Elevation

1 Entrance to Corporate Office
2 Mosque
3 Evaporative Cooling Tower
4 Roof Canopy Over Roof Garden
5 Entrance Canopy

The whole is served by three major basement levels of car-parking, which are connected by lifts and escalators to the retail & office levels above. On the north-eastern corner, Yeang has proposed

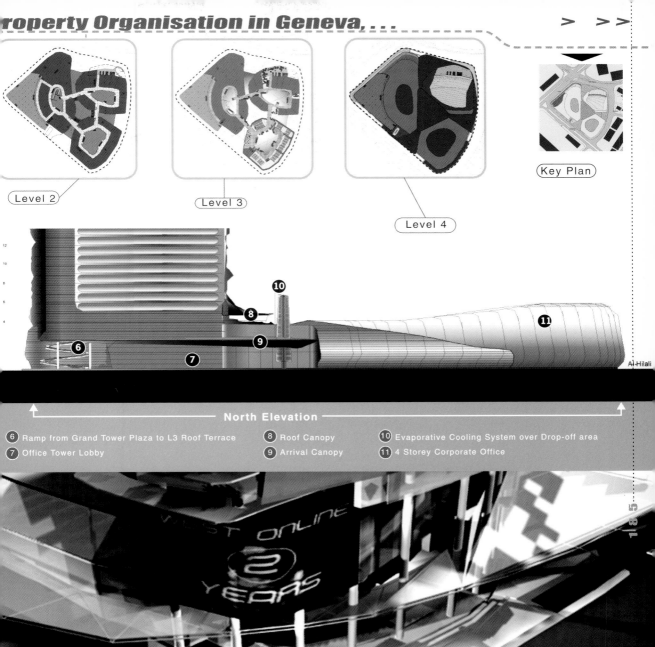

Level 2

Level 3

Level 4

Key Plan

Al-Hilali

North Elevation

⑥ Ramp from Grand Tower Plaza to L3 Roof Terrace ⑧ Roof Canopy ⑩ Evaporative Cooling System over Drop-off area

⑦ Office Tower Lobby ⑨ Arrival Canopy ⑪ 4 Storey Corporate Office

a slim signature office tower with bioclimatic design elements. The main office floors face north for waterfront views, while the slim east and west facades reduce solar gain, and the major service and elevator cores shield the southern face of the tower. The office tower is wrapped with sunshading screens which fold out to form a canopy over a roof garden on the southern roof-podium. The southern facade is also veiled with a planted green inner layer and the north facade incorporates sky terraces with planting. While a predominantly retail brief with commercial office space is essentially limited in scope, Yeang has enlivened the whole proposition with the idea of human scale; the Retail Villages. Then, a series of sectional studies for shading, natural ventilation of the shopping streets and innovative roof forms bring a fresh bioclimatic layer to the whole project. Proposals for rainwater collection, irrigation and planting, and the recycling of waste are also included. The most inventive three-dimensional section options are those for wind and solar massing which offer a basis for extensive detail design and development. The evaporative cooling towers are also part of this advancing discipline of air movement and cooling, which in itself is deeply rooted in tradition and response to climate.

1 Tiered Seating Overlooking Plaza   2 Media Screen - 24hr Promotion

Internal Perspective View

beijing world
trade

2.1 2.2 2.3 2.4 2.5 2.6 2.7 2.8 2.9 2.10 2.11 2.12 2

ch

9.21 Ha gross (apartments)173 582sq.m.(offices) 255 200sq.m.(hotel & convention centre) 45 580sq.m.

(service apartments) 11 320sq.m. (retail & commercial) 14 000sq.m. (cultural plaza & green belt park) 33 858sq.m. (carparking & circulation) 146 300sq.m.

science &
centre :

.14 2.15 2.16 2.17 2.18 2.19 2.20 2.21 2.22 2.23 2.24 2.25

3.13.2 3.3 credits

ina

g Kong International Development Co. Ltd. Client 40°N Latitude 23, East Sanhuan North Road, Chaoyang District, Beijing, P. R. China Location **Project Data** ▬

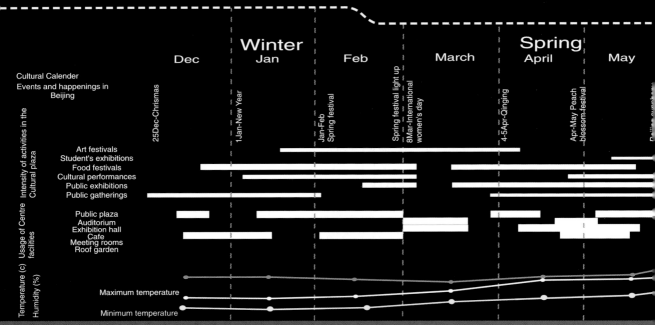

			Winter				Spring	
		Dec	Jan	Feb	March	April	May

Cultural Calender
Events and happenings in Beijing

25Dec-Chrismas · 1Jan-New Year · Jan-Feb Spring festival · Spring festival light up · 8Mar-International women's day · 4-5Apr-Qinging · Apr-May Peach blossom-festival

Intensity of activities in the Cultural plaza

Art festivals
Student's exhibitions
Food festivals
Cultural performances
Public exhibitions
Public gatherings

Usage of Centre facilities

Public plaza
Auditorium
Exhibition hall
Cafe
Meeting rooms
Roof garden

Temperature (c) Humidity (%)

Maximum temperature

Minimum temperature

This massive urban structure occupies a set of city-blocks and is essentially a subscraper with a central Plaza, surrounded by office and apartment towers on its east and west frontages. The dominant ecological feature of the development is in the form of a linear (green belt park) which extends from the western corner of the site, on street level, and connects to all parts of the development via landscaped

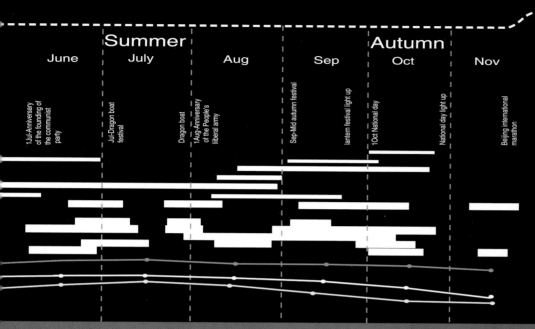

	Summer				Autumn		
June	July	Aug	Sep	Oct	Nov		

1Jul-Anniversary of the founding of the communist party

1Jul-Dragon boat festival

Dragon boat

1Aug-Anniversary of the People's lliberal army

Sep-Mid autumn festival

lantern festival light up

1Oct National day

National day light up

Beijing international marathon

ramps and bridges. These extend into the lower levels of the office towers, which also contain a variety of skycourts. The brief called for a landmark public facility, planned as a self contained (24 Hour CBD) mini city, and designed as a microcosm of the larger city. The mixed development includes an integrated range of facilities including business offices, hotel, apartments, cultural and recreation functions.

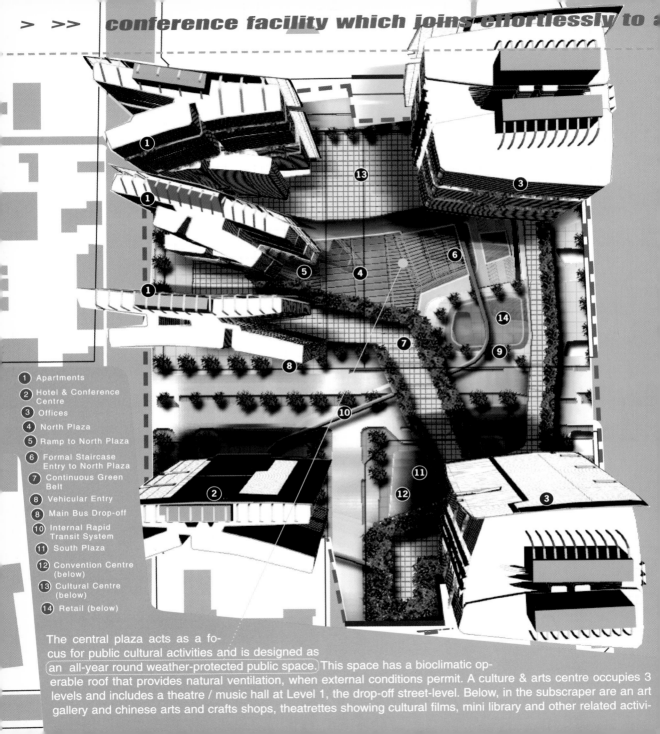

1. Apartments
2. Hotel & Conference Centre
3. Offices
4. North Plaza
5. Ramp to North Plaza
6. Formal Staircase Entry to North Plaza
7. Continuous Green Belt
8. Vehicular Entry
8. Main Bus Drop-off
10. Internal Rapid Transit System
11. South Plaza
12. Convention Centre (below)
13. Cultural Centre (below)
14. Retail (below)

The central plaza acts as a focus for public cultural activities and is designed as an all-year round weather-protected public space. This space has a bioclimatic operable roof that provides natural ventilation, when external conditions permit. A culture & arts centre occupies 3 levels and includes a theatre / music hall at Level 1, the drop-off street-level. Below, in the subscraper are an art gallery and chinese arts and crafts shops, theatrettes showing cultural films, mini library and other related activi-

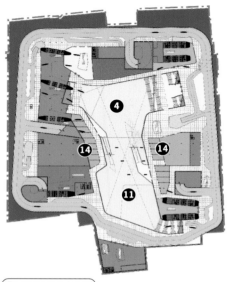

(Basement 1 Level)

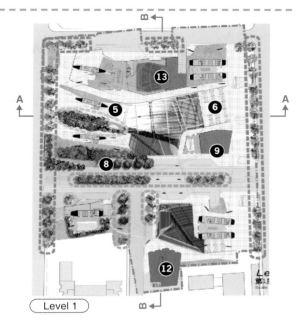

(Level 1)

(Level 2)

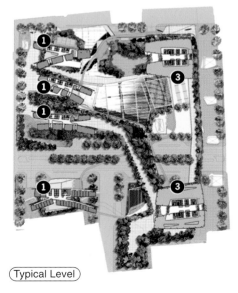

(Typical Level)

Section AA

These in turn open out, on level B2, to the cultural plaza, which houses various outdoor cultural events for the festivals and celebrations in Beijing. A convention centre & hotel are a dual-function integrated facility. The convention centre is predominantly below street level and faces the cultural plaza to its north. The topmost floor, at street level is an Expo pavilion, which can be combined with the convention centre for larger conference and exhibition events. A retail centre is also included and forms part of the pedestrian circulation route, again encircling the cultural plaza, and connecting to all other buildings within the over-all development. The project relies heavily on the provision of horizontal and vertical linkages, pedes-trianisation, and the inclusion of an internal rapid transit system for express movement of users.

Section BB

The towers are structured on a series of Yeang's bioclimatic principles. The apartments are slim-plan for daylighting, views and cross ventilation. Each apartment has a garden terrace with adjustable glass shutters that enclose the space in winter, as a green house, while in summer they are opened up to encourage natural cooling. The paired Gateway Office Towers have a split-plan with atria. Large movable vertical screen-blades between, at atrium ends, modify the internal environment by deflecting or scooping wind into the atrium space. Essentially, the complexity of the programme and Yeang's ecological response is simplified by using the subscraper as a collector of culture, commerce and plaza, the overlayering of the linear park, while leaving the towers to define the skyline, infused with sky-courts and landscaping.

East 3rd Ring Road

Guandongdiannan Street

(1) Apartments
(2) Hotel & Conference Centre
(3) Offices
(4) North Plaza
(5) Ramp to North Plaza
(6) Formal Staircase Entry to North Plaza
(7) Continuous Greeen Belt
(8) Vehicular Entry
(9) Main Bus Drop-off
(10) Internal Rapid Transit System
(11) South Plaza
(12) Convention Centre (below)
(13) Cultural Centre (below)
(14) Retail (below)

2.1 2.2 2.3 2.4 2.5 2.6 2.7 2.8 2.9 2.10 2.11 2.12 2

(7 apartment towers) 35 storeys (2 hotel towers) 50 storeys (4 hotel blocks) 15 storeys

jabal omar

(retail concourse) 4 storeys no.ofstoreys 232 000sq.m SiteArea   prayer terraces and landscaped gardens: 94 000sq.m. carparking: 309 00

crystalline form.

Masjid Al Haram

3.1 3.2 3.3 c r e d i t s

masterplan:

ca

gross: 878 880 sq.m. nett: 565 650 sq.m. Areas   Makkah Construction and Development Company Client   Mecca, Saudi Arabia Location **— Project Data —**

199

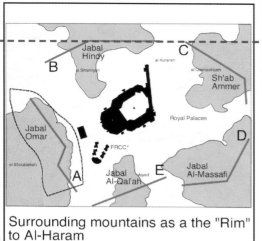

Surrounding mountains as a the "Rim" to Al-Haram

Jabal Hindy

Jabal Omar

al Koraráh

al Shamiyah

al Oranaaitiyeh

Sh'ab Ammer

Royal Palaces

FRCC*

Jabal Al-Qal'ah

el Shoubiekah

Aiyad

Jabal Al-Massafi

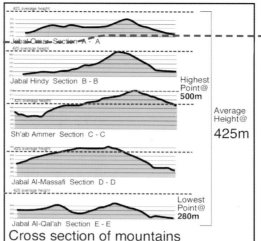

Jabal Omar Section A - A

Jabal Hindy Section B - B

Sh'ab Ammer Section C - C

Jabal Al-Massafi Section D - D

Jabal Al-Qal'ah Section E - E

Cross section of mountains

Highest Point @ 500m

Average Height @ 425m

Lowest Point @ 280m

Elevation

The overall design concept starts from Yeang's topographical study of the five principal mountains which encircle the valley of Al-Haram, establishing a rim of mountain ridges. Three peaks that make up the Jabal Omar site form the western edge of this enclosure, or rim, defining the development. A concourse runs the length of the ridge line taking advantage of the elevated position from which the Al-Haram can be seen.

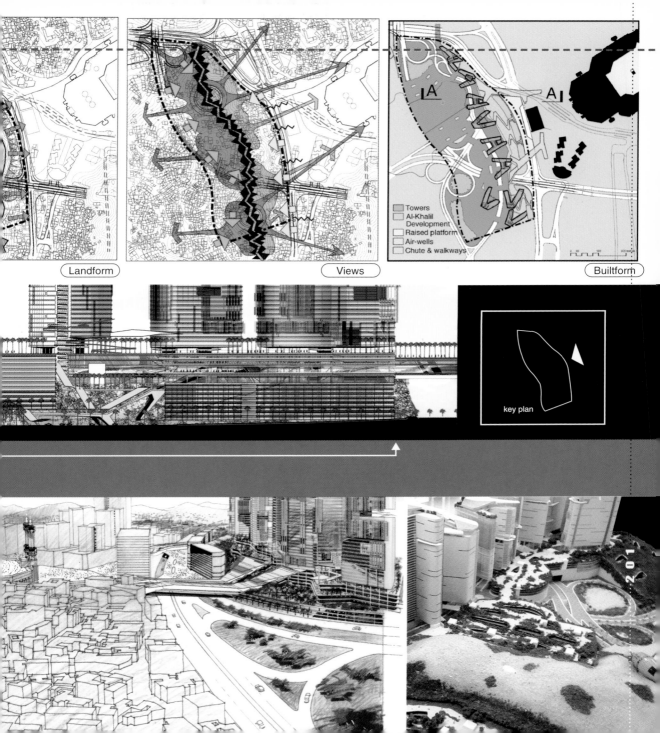

Landform

Views

Builtform

Towers
Al-Khalil Development
Raised platform
Air-wells
Chute & walkways

key plan

201

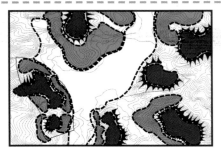

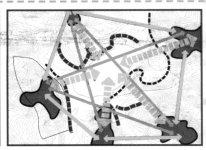

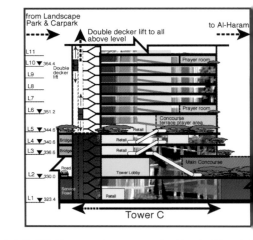

from Landscape Park & Carpark

to Al-Haram

Double decker lift to all above level

L11
L10 ▼364.4
L9
L8 — Double decker lift
L7
L6 ▼351.2
L5 ▼344.6
L4 ▼340.6
L3 ▼336.6
L2 ▼330.0
L1 ▼323.4

Prayer room

Prayer room

Concourse terrace prayer area

Retail
Retail
Retail

Bridge
Bridge

Road

Main Concourse

Tower Lobby

Service Road

Retail

Tower C

Yeang's detail design is then based upon a linear green park, extending the length of the site, in order to create a calming, natural environment for the pilgrims. This transformation of the site into a green groundscraper creates exten-

Moulded carpak with 'green' bridges linkages

Service road entry

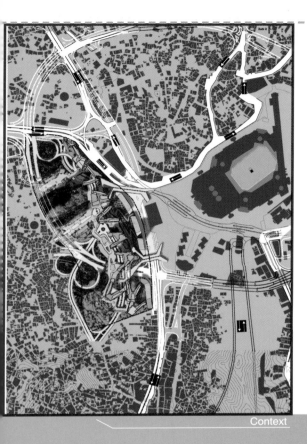

Context

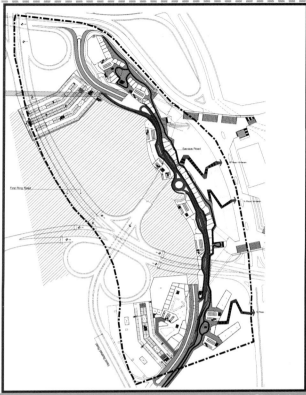

Service Road Level Circulation

-sive, shaded external spaces with [palm trees] and other indigenous vegetation, which require minimal water for irrigation. The water supply for the greening of the site comes from the conserved grey water of the development. The key to the design lies in the cross-section, which reveals the extensive trees and planting at the roof level of the buried ground-form, the planting at

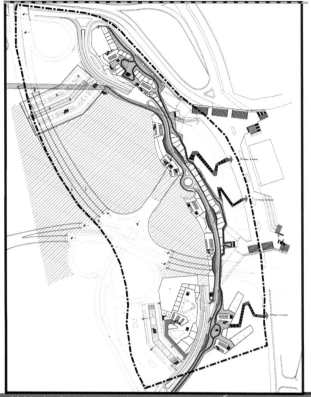

Podium Roof Garden as usable Spaces

main concourse level and the landscaped roof of the carparking on the western slope. This is augmented by palm tree planting on eastern slopes, facing Al-Haram Yeang's vision of a sea of green. Above this green land form the apartment towers rise in a series of 'A', 'V', 'H' & 'M' plan-form typologies, with maxi-

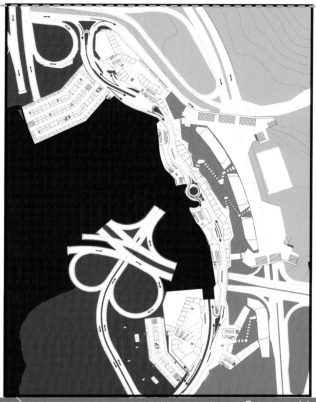

Concourse L1

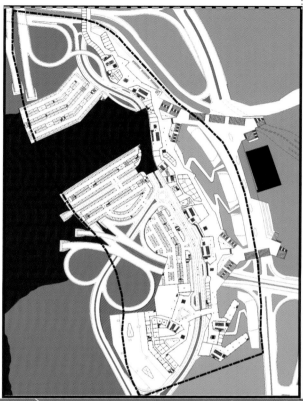

Main Concourse [L2]

Pedestrian Chute directs Pilgrims towards the Al-Haram

Connection between main Concourse and Pedestrian Chute

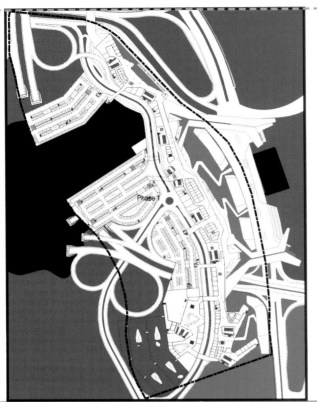

L3

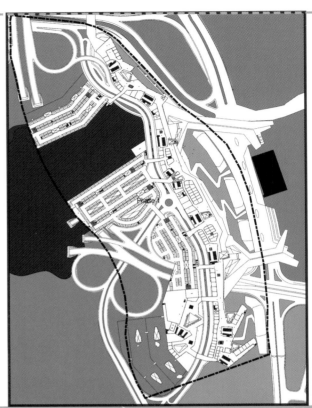

L4

Sectional View of Model

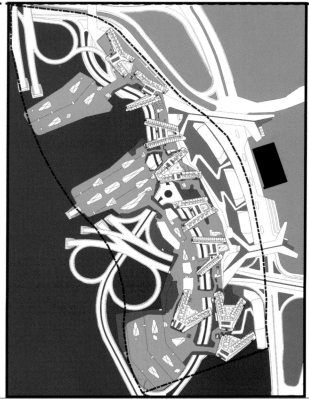

Typical Level [L8]

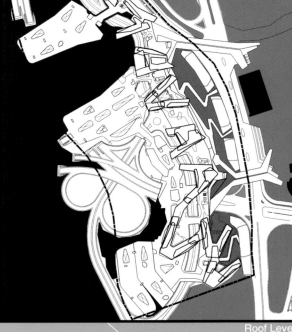

Roof Level

maximum facade area and views to Al-Haram. The towers are marked by windscoops and evaporative cooling shafts, which provide passive low-energy-cooling, for user-comfort. This passive system has been extensively studied in the engineering of the design, together with sunshading and other bioclimatic features.

At the outset, Yeang defined the principal design considerations as speed of accessibility to Al-Haram during prayer call, and views affordability from apartment units and hotel suites to the point of pilgrimage, Al-Haram itself. This is coupled with the need to accommodate a high population density of pilgrims and their mission of prayer. The tower typologies satisfy the conditions for views, as do the prayer platforms and roof gardens. Then, the central concourse promenade acts as a collector for the various public transport systems, defined as chutes to Al-Haram. A combination of elevators, escalators, travelators and walking are integrated together to reduce the travel time between residential

Bridge Link 2 from Al-Haram

suite and the Al-Haram, via covered chutes and bridges to the forecourt. A travel-time analysis demonstrates the modes and times, together with other factors such as sight-line analysis from the towers to Al-Haram and associated spaces for prayers from within the towers, and without in the plaza around the Al-Haram all are clear generators of the design. The Parkland-Ridge as a groundscraper base for the inhabited spine of towers, forms a green-oasis in the harsh climate of a hot arid zone.

al-hilali com

al-hilali com

al-hilali c

al-hilali complex

complex

al-hilali complex

al-hila

al-hilali co

al-hilali complex

13 000sq.m (overall) 4 000sq.m (commercial complex)Sit

al-hilali complex

plex: kuwait

al-hilali complex

city

al-hilali complex

al-hilali complex

al-hilali comp

al-hilali comp

complex

oreys + 1 mezannine floor no. of storeys gross: 32 044sq.m. nett: 24 755sq.m. Areas Kuwait Real Estate Company Client Kuwait City Location **—Project Data —**

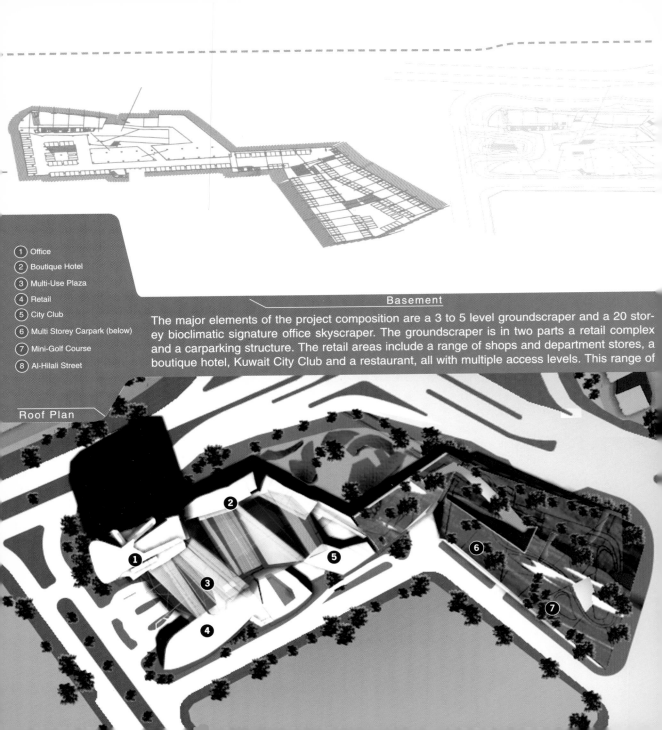

1. Office
2. Boutique Hotel
3. Multi-Use Plaza
4. Retail
5. City Club
6. Multi Storey Carpark (below)
7. Mini-Golf Course
8. Al-Hilali Street

Basement

The major elements of the project composition are a 3 to 5 level groundscraper and a 20 storey bioclimatic signature office skyscraper. The groundscraper is in two parts a retail complex and a carparking structure. The retail areas include a range of shops and department stores, a boutique hotel, Kuwait City Club and a restaurant, all with multiple access levels. This range of

Roof Plan

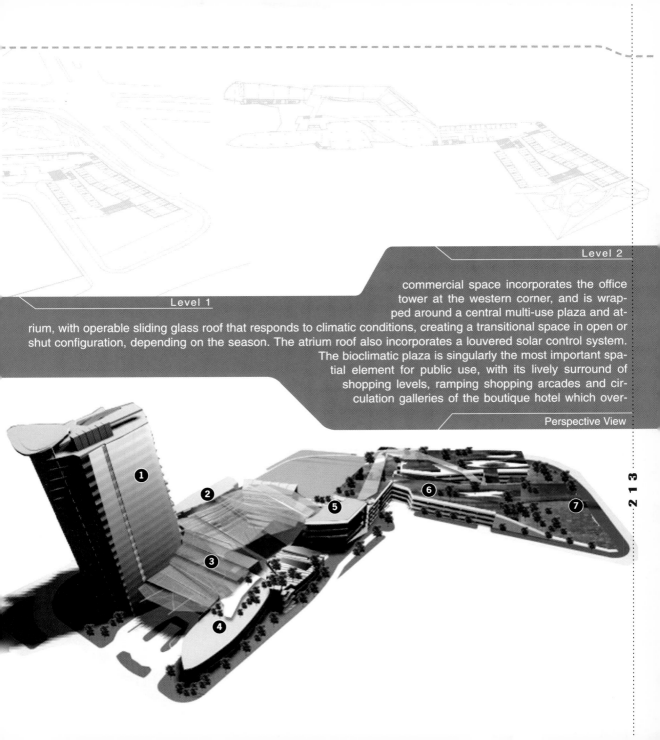

commercial space incorporates the office tower at the western corner, and is wrapped around a central multi-use plaza and atrium, with operable sliding glass roof that responds to climatic conditions, creating a transitional space in open or shut configuration, depending on the season. The atrium roof also incorporates a louvered solar control system. The bioclimatic plaza is singularly the most important spatial element for public use, with its lively surround of shopping levels, ramping shopping arcades and circulation galleries of the boutique hotel which over-

Level 1

Perspective View

hotel which overlook the plaza. The fact that it is a semi outdoor space with seasonal variation adds a further dimension which changes the spatial condition and its tempered environment. The plaza and food court areas incorporate water features and planting which contribute to a cooler environment, and the retail areas incorporate a chimney-core system as part of the overall environmental strategy.

Sectional View of Model

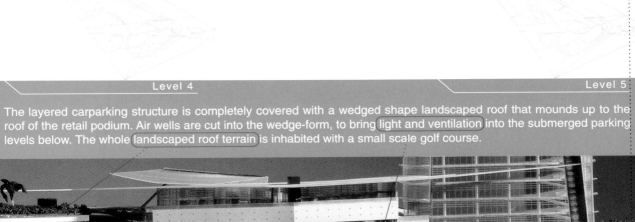

The layered carparking structure is completely covered with a wedged shape landscaped roof that mounds up to the roof of the retail podium. Air wells are cut into the wedge-form, to bring light and ventilation into the submerged parking levels below. The whole landscaped roof terrain is inhabited with a small scale golf course.

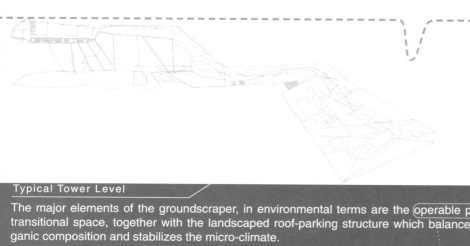

Typical Tower Level

The major elements of the groundscraper, in environmental terms are the (operable plaza roof) and the creation of transitional space, together with the landscaped roof-parking structure which balances the site's inorganic and organic composition and stabilizes the micro-climate.

Boutique Hotel

Entrance

Yeang's signature office skyscraper similarly incorporates a whole range of elements which are part of his green / bioclimatic skyscraper agenda. In this case the sunpath adaptation incorporates double-skin flue walls, as a ventilating space, on west and east facades. These flue walls exhaust air as ventilation through the facade construction and minimise solar heat gain. Service cores are grouped into a solar shield wall on the south facade, while the north facade incorporates full height clear glazed curtain walling. The site specific sun-shading devices are also included, together with transitional-space skycourts with planting and landscaping.

The whole project in itself is transitional, as it demonstrates the growth of Yeang's bioclimatic design into a larger ecological design agenda and the evolution of the sustainable intensive urban building, as a new typology.

Multi-Use Plaza

BATC - business technology

ess advanced
centre

1.8 Msq.ft Site Area gross: 7.62 Msq.ft. nett: 5.71 Msq.ft.　Areas　　TRC Development Sdn Bhd Client　　Lot 4582, Mukim of Setapak, Kuala Lumpur Location ▬Project Data ▬

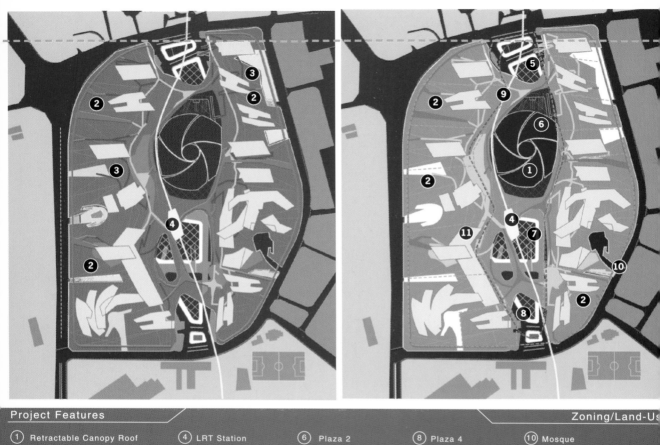

Project Features

1. Retractable Canopy Roof
2. Public Green Park
3. Sky Walks
4. LRT Station
5. Plaza 1
6. Plaza 2
7. Plaza 3
8. Plaza 4
8. IRTS Line
10. Mosque
11. Cyber Tech Centre

Zoning/Land-Us[e]

Cross-Section

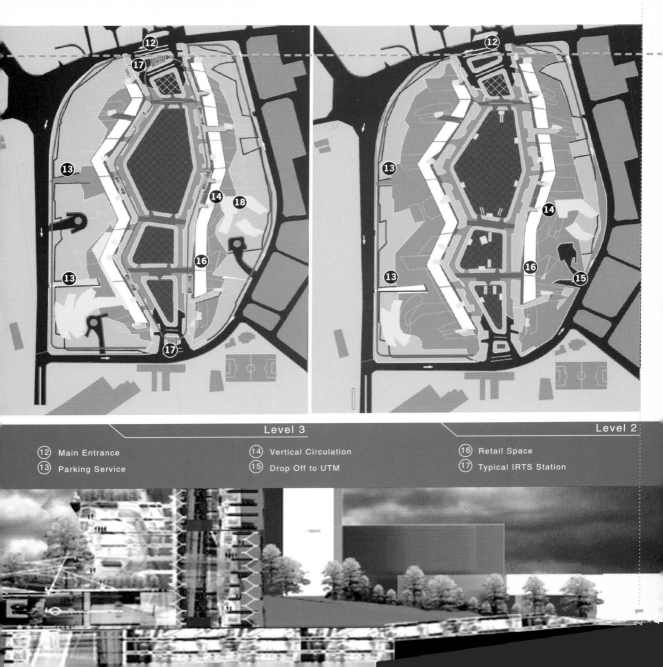

Level 3   Level 2

12 Main Entrance   14 Vertical Circulation   16 Retail Space

13 Parking Service   15 Drop Off to UTM   17 Typical IRTS Station

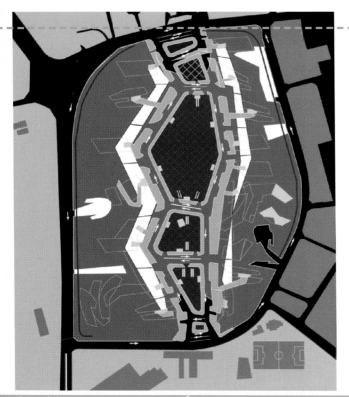

Level 1

View through the Central Events Plaza

Masjid

The project for the University Teknologi Malaysia, incorporates both educational facilities, Research and Development and electronic-commerce related activities. This development is thus a Branch Campus of UTM and a Satellite to the Multimedia Super Corridor.

Yeang's central principle is the creation of a Parkland a mounded man-made landform, inhabited at its linear centre by retail street-strips that surround a series of multi-use urban squares. The largest of these is designed as an Event Plaza with a retractable canopy roof.

The Groundscraper is thus expressed as a major park landform, mounded to reduce its impact on the surrounding area. The site is bounded by major roads and is traversed by the raised LRT system. Within this island of park-space, Yeang has placed a series of

The Garden Mosque is located within the Prime Central Space

| Basement | L1 | L2 |

Towers which are grouped towards the spinal centre, together with a signature tower, in order to give visual priority to the Park itself as a major surround of public greenspace. Water gardens and soft landscaping enhance the Pedestrian routes throughout the site.

Yeang's concept of buildings in the park is drawn directly from his ecological design principles, in this case enhancing the organic content of the urban eco-system by the introduction of a major parkland setting. Pedestrian and Landscape Bridges form important linkages across the site and the massive range of high-rise forms.

The main facilities are linked by a boulevard that is vehicle-free, with covered public walkways. An air-conditioned Internal Rapid Transit System is also incorporated for ease of connection.

The major towers are all based on Yeang's bioclimatic design principles, as are the Plazas and related facilities.

The signature tower has been developed into a detail design which exhibits all the intensive ecological characteristics of Yeang's green skyscraper series, along with his innovative principles of Vertical Urbanism. This incorporates important skycourt spatial linkages, together with Vertical Landscaping, parks and squares.

The parkland-mounded-groundscraper pierced by the Events Plaza, provides a massive organic ground-plane for the vertically-greened Towers, forming a sustainable ecological whole a civilized oasis of nature, within the intensive city of Kuala Lumpur.

View from Main Public Plaza

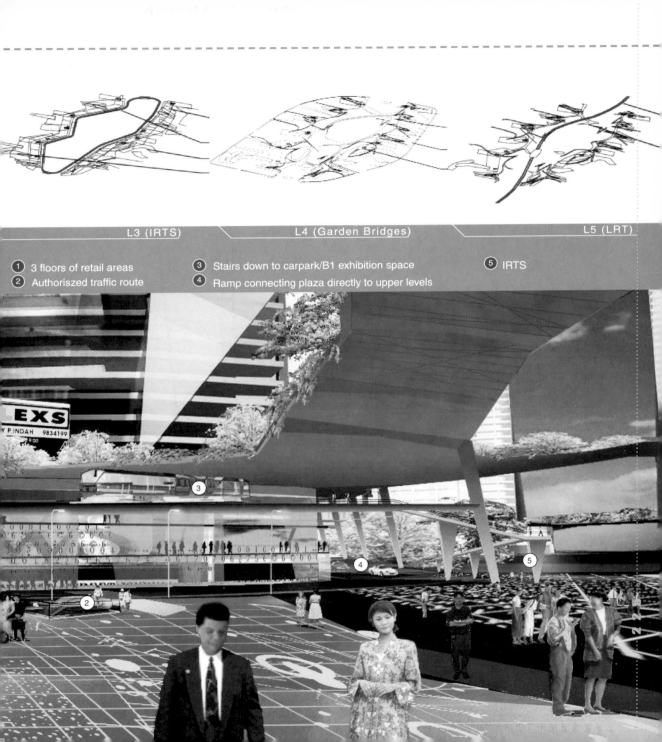

L3 (IRTS)   L4 (Garden Bridges)   L5 (LRT)

1. 3 floors of retail areas
2. Authorsized traffic route
3. Stairs down to carpark/B1 exhibition space
4. Ramp connecting plaza directly to upper levels
5. IRTS

haikou masterplan

64 Hectares SiteArea 20 storeys observation tow

urban park
: china

Municipal Council of Haikou City Client   Haikou City, Hainan, China Location   **Project Data**

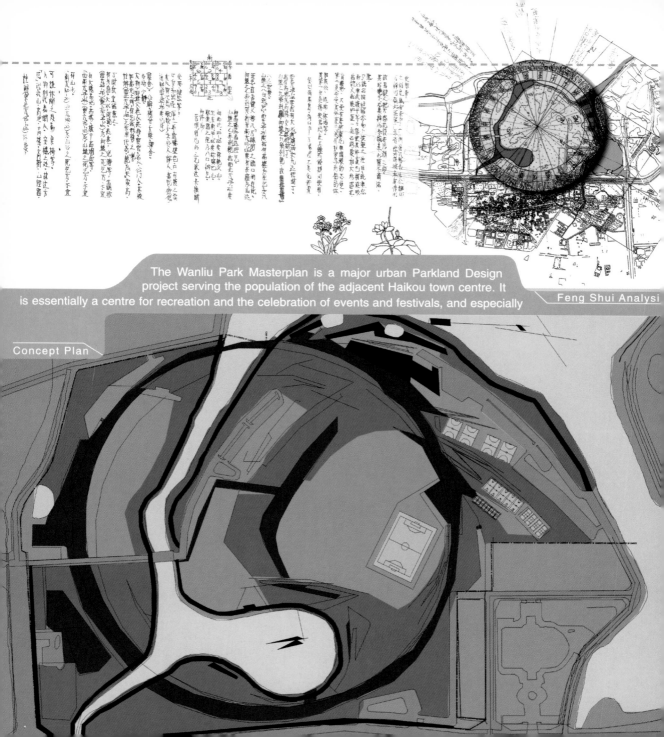

The Wanliu Park Masterplan is a major urban Parkland Design project serving the population of the adjacent Haikou town centre. It is essentially a centre for recreation and the celebration of events and festivals, and especially

Concept Plan

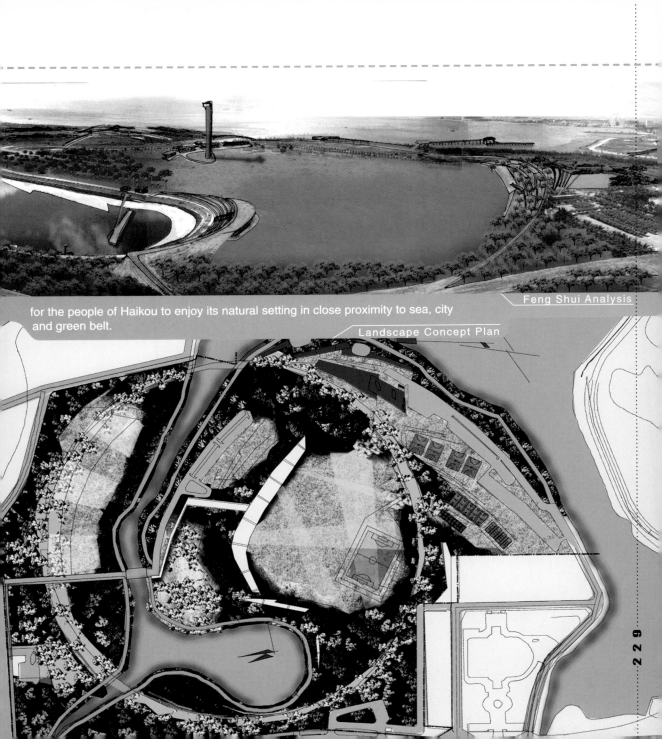

Feng Shui Analysis

for the people of Haikou to enjoy its natural setting in close proximity to sea, city and green belt.

Landscape Concept Plan

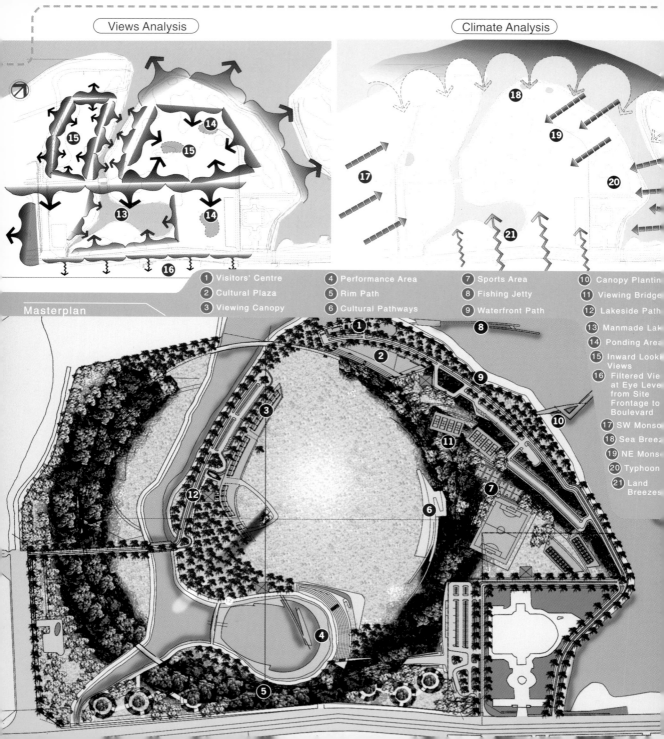

Views Analysis

Climate Analysis

Masterplan

1 Visitors' Centre
2 Cultural Plaza
3 Viewing Canopy
4 Performance Area
5 Rim Path
6 Cultural Pathways
7 Sports Area
8 Fishing Jetty
9 Waterfront Path
10 Canopy Plantin
11 Viewing Bridge
12 Lakeside Path
13 Manmade Lak
14 Ponding Area
15 Inward Looki
Views
16 Filtered Vie
at Eye Leve
from Site
Frontage to
Boulevard
17 SW Monso
18 Sea Breez
19 NE Monso
20 Typhoon
21 Land
Breezes

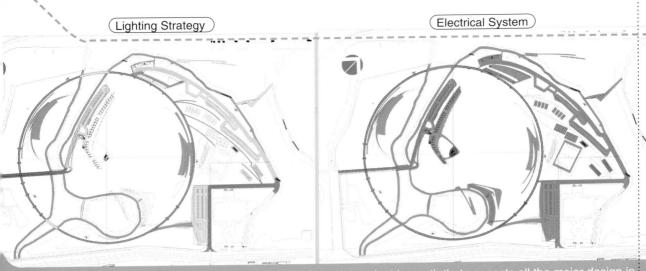

The various elements of the masterplan are unified by a circular pedestrian path that connects all the major design installations in the park. One major vertical structure serves both as a 20 storey viewing tower, with views to Haikou City, and also acts as a windmill. Coastal water elements are enhanced in the masterplan with a performance island, artificial beach, a fishing jetty, viewing bridges and seafront promenades.

The local Chinese culture is represented by annual festivals including local coconut festival, mooncake festival and valentine festival with dedicated planting areas or feature pathways designed into the Park. The overall proposition amounts to a huge landscape park with a wide ranging landscaping strategy and series of integrated structures and pathways, each with a particular focus. Seen as a whole, the architecture of the groundscraper is the whole encircled landform and its series of pavilion forms and other facilities, taken together. For instance the landscaping provides large canopy planting for sunshading during hot weather, and wind breakers are strategically planted to protect park and sports areas from coastal winds. A mangrove swamp is included in the coastal area to give bio-diversity to the water based vegetation.

Amongst the twenty four site installations, which surround a huge open-air lawn, are a Cultural Plaza for Women's

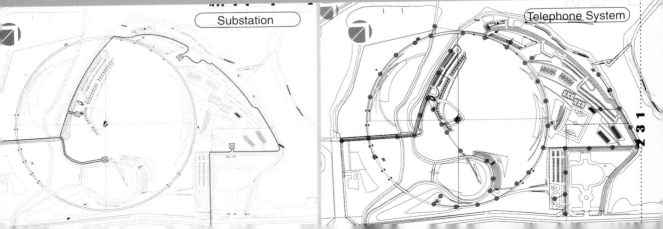

Fishing Jetty Plan

Visitor's Centre Section

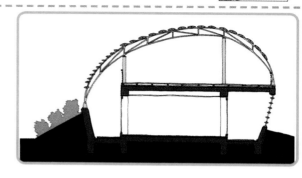

Fishing Jetty Section

Day and Children's Day Festival performances. This is associated with a visitor's centre, a two-storey curvi-linear extrusion with naturally ventilated first-floor viewing gallery and promenade covered in an adjustable metal louvre roof, with cafe, exhibition hall and gift shop beneath. Conversely, the Mooncake Festival Path is not a building but a series of landform elements which include a ramp promenade, festival plaza and a lantern planting and seating wall. A performance island, artificial beach and arena seating are a further prominent landform surrounding water, while the viewing bridge which connects two parks across a river inlet exemplifies a free-standing structure, to be illuminated at night as a gateway landmark. Yeang's ecological agenda is extensive. It includes canopy sunshading and cross ventilation to grandstand seating, strategic planting to enhance ecological balance, and solar panels to generate stored electricity for footpath lighting. The viewing tower generates its own wind-powered electricity supply, and grey water is collected and recycled into park services.

The project has some precedent in Spain, but the coastal element and the Chinese culture make it unique, regional-ecological.

Changing Room Section

Changing Room Elevation

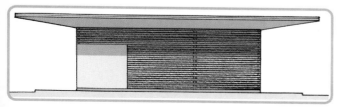
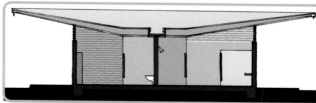
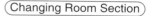

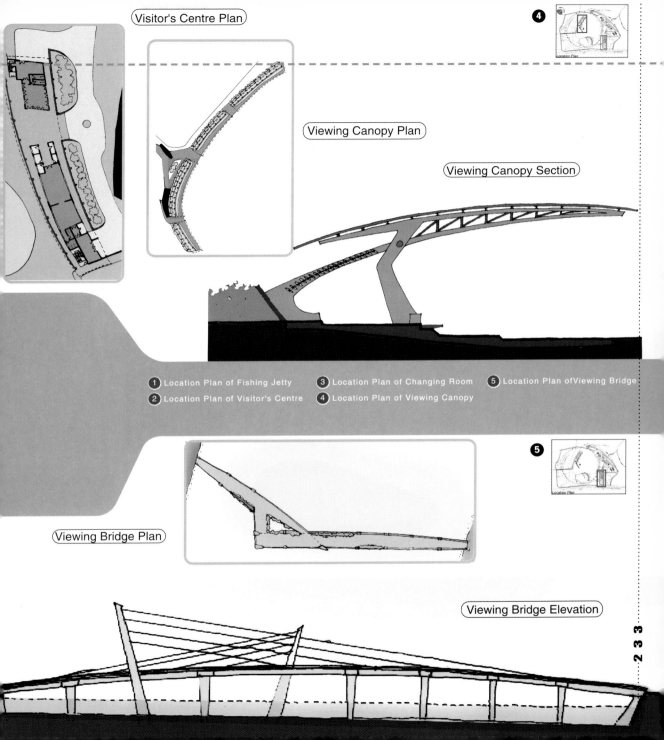

Visitor's Centre Plan

Viewing Canopy Plan

Viewing Canopy Section

1 Location Plan of Fishing Jetty   3 Location Plan of Changing Room   5 Location Plan of Viewing Bridge
2 Location Plan of Visitor's Centre   4 Location Plan of Viewing Canopy

Viewing Bridge Plan

Viewing Bridge Elevation

HIPA
masterplan

75 acres (30 hectares acres)SiteArea

township
: laos

-3 storeys (max.) no.ofstoreys/heights   HIPA Corporation Sdn Bhd Client   17.58° N Latitude   Vientianne, Laos Location ▬ **Project Data** ▬

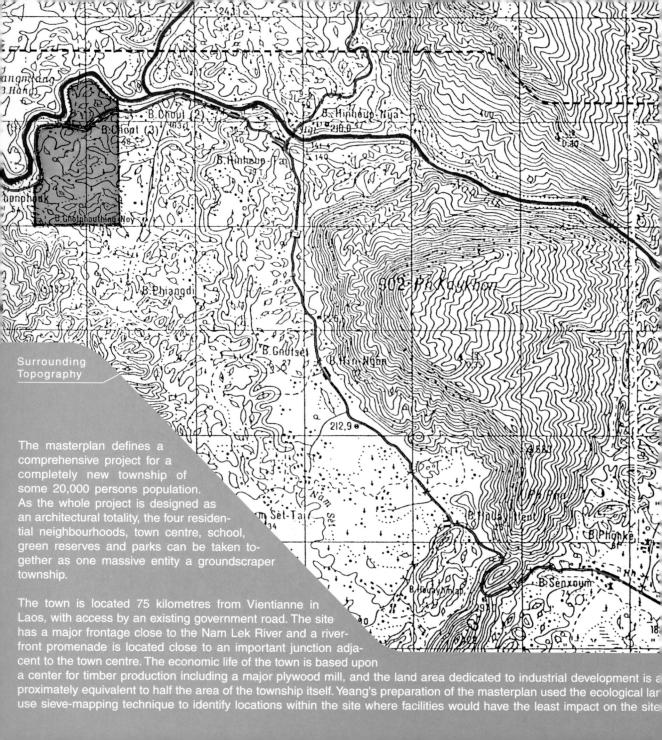

The masterplan defines a
comprehensive project for a
completely new township of
some 20,000 persons population.
As the whole project is designed as
an architectural totality, the four residential neighbourhoods, town centre, school,
green reserves and parks can be taken together as one massive entity a groundscraper
township.

The town is located 75 kilometres from Vientianne in
Laos, with access by an existing government road. The site
has a major frontage close to the Nam Lek River and a riverfront promenade is located close to an important junction adjacent to the town centre. The economic life of the town is based upon
a center for timber production including a major plywood mill, and the land area dedicated to industrial development is a
proximately equivalent to half the area of the township itself. Yeang's preparation of the masterplan used the ecological lar
use sieve-mapping technique to identify locations within the site where facilities would have the least impact on the site

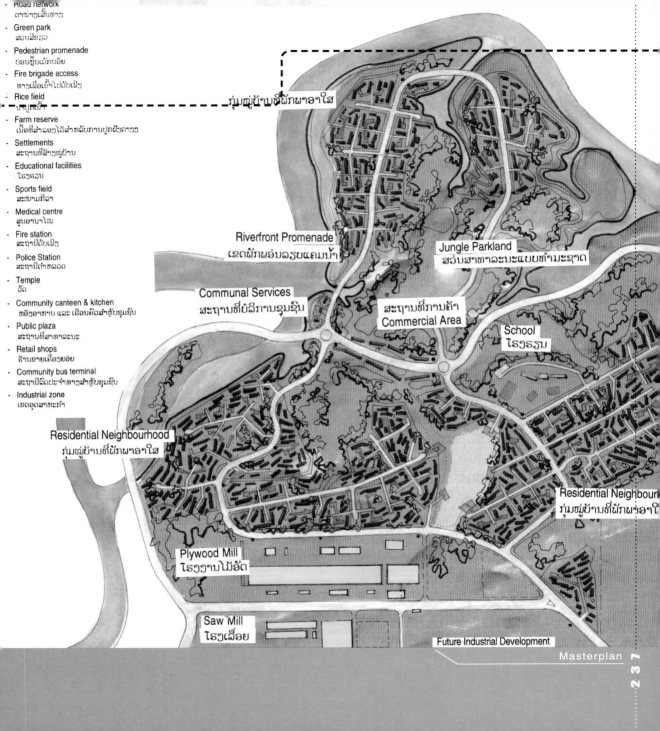

- Road network
  ຕາຂ່າຍເສັ້ນທາງ
- Green park
  ສວນສີຂຽວ
- Pedestrian promenade
  ບ່ອນຍ່ຽນໜ້າ.ບັໄຍ
- Fire brigade access
  ທາງເພື່ອເຂົ້າໄປດັບເພີງ
- Rice field
  ນາກະສຳ
- Farm reserve
  ເນື້ອທີ່ສຳລອງໄວ້ສຳຫລັບການປູກຝັງຕ່າງໆ
- Settlements
  ສະຖານທີ່ສ້າງໝູ່ບ້ານ
- Educational facilities
  ໂຮງຮຽນ
- Sports field
  ສະໜາມກິລາ
- Medical centre
  ສູນອານາໄມ
- Fire station
  ສະຖານີດັບເພີງ
- Police Station
  ສະຖານີຕຳຫລວດ
- Temple
  ວັດ
- Community canteen & kitchen
  ຫ້ອງອາຫານ ແລະ ເຮືອນຄົວສຳຫຼັບຊຸມຊົນ
- Public plaza
  ສະຖານທີ່ສາທາລະນະ
- Retail shops
  ຮ້ານຂາຍເຄື່ອງຍ່ອຍ
- Community bus terminal
  ສະຖານີລົດປະຈຳທາງສຳຫຼັບຊຸມຊົນ
- Industrial zone
  ເຂດອຸດສາຫະກຳ

ກຸ່ມໝູ່ບ້ານທີ່ພັກຜາອາໃສ

Riverfront Promenade
ເຂດຜັກຜ່ອນລຽບແຄມນ້ຳ

Jungle Parkland
ສວນສາທາລະນະແບບທຳມະຊາດ

Communal Services
ສະຖານທີ່ບໍລິການຂຸມຊົນ

ສະຖານທີ່ການຄ້າ
Commercial Area

School
ໂຮງຮຽນ

Residential Neighbourhood
ກຸ່ມໝູ່ບ້ານທີ່ພັກຜາອາໃສ

Residential Neighbour
ກຸ່ມໝູ່ບ້ານທີ່ພັກຜ່ອາໃ

Plywood Mill
ໂຮງງານໄມ້ອັດ

Saw Mill
ໂຮງເລື່ອຍ

Future Industrial Development

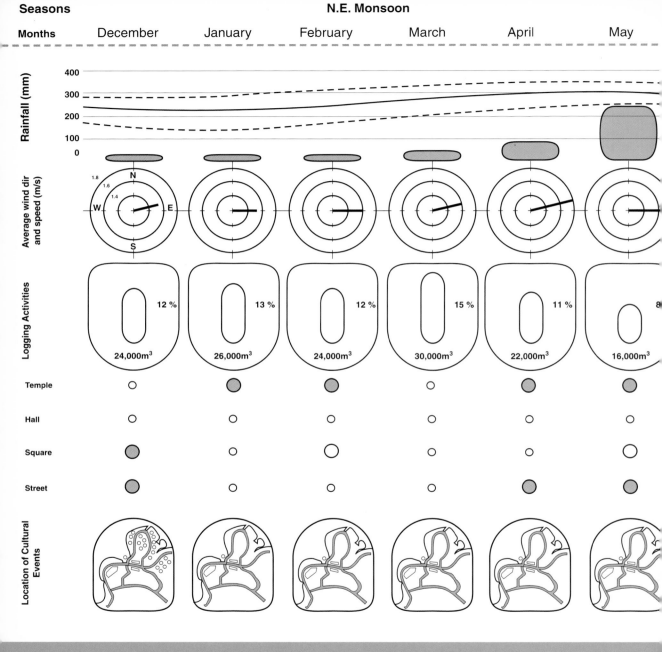

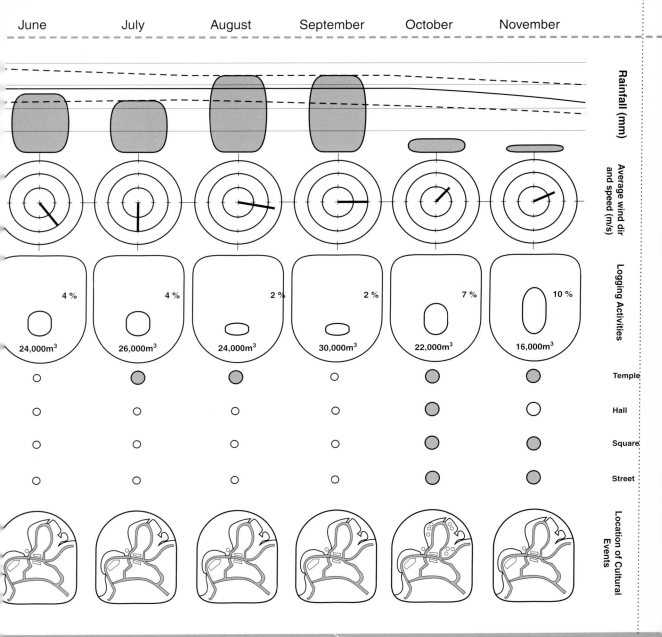

June	July	August	September	October	November

Rainfall (mm)

Average wind dir and speed (m/s)

Logging Activities

| 4 % | 4 % | 2 % | 2 % | 7 % | 10 % |
| 24,000m³ | 26,000m³ | 24,000m³ | 30,000m³ | 22,000m³ | 16,000m³ |

Temple

Hall

Square

Street

Location of Cultural Events

sites and retains the existing topography and vegetation patterns. This includes a substantial area of conserved jungle parkland at the core of the settlement, together with a rice field and other ground cover.

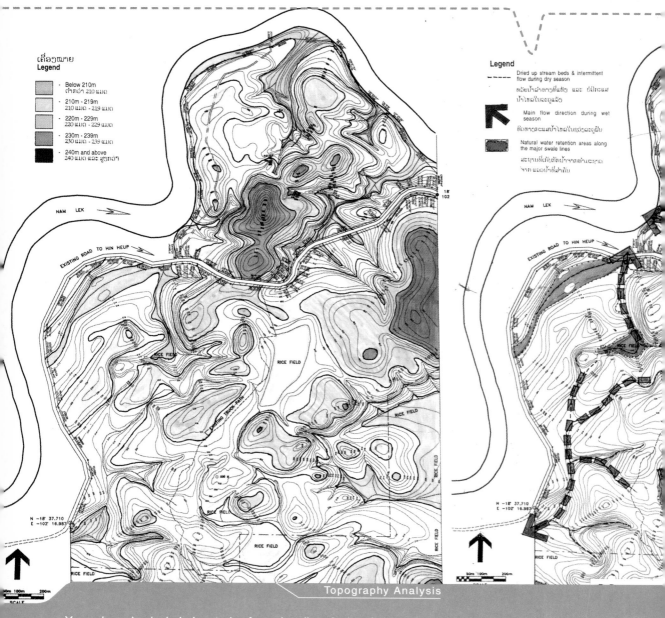

Legend / เคื่อງໝາຍ

- Below 210m / ຕ່ຳກວ່າ 210 ແມດ
- 210m - 219m / 210 ແມດ - 219 ແມດ
- 220m - 229m / 220 ແມດ - 229 ແມດ
- 230m - 239m / 230 ແມດ - 239 ແມດ
- 240m and above / 240 ແມດ ແລະ ສູງກວ່າ")

Legend

- Dried up stream beds & intermittent flow during dry season / ໜ້ວຍນ້ຳລຳຫ້ວຍທີ່ແຫ້ງ ແລະ ບໍ່ມີກະແສ ນ້ຳໄຫລໃນລະດູແລ້ງ
- Main flow direction during wet season / ຕິດທາງລະແມກນ້ຳໄຫລໃນຊ່ວງລະດູຝົນ
- Natural water retention areas along the major swale lines / ພະຍາບໍ່ໃນທີ່ເກັບກັກນ້ຳຈາກທາງລະດູກາດ ຈາກ ແອ່ງນ້ຳທີ່ຕໍ່ກັນ

NAM LEK

EXISTING ROAD TO HIN HEUP

RICE FIELD

N –18° 37.710
E –102° 16.987

18' 102

SCALE

Topography Analysis

Yeang has also included a study of species diversity in relation to latitude, in this case the swallow-tail butterflies, and the incidence is very high in this regional latitude strengthening the case for conservation of natural habitat. An annual cultural activities calendar related to NE and SW monsoon seasons is also included, to-

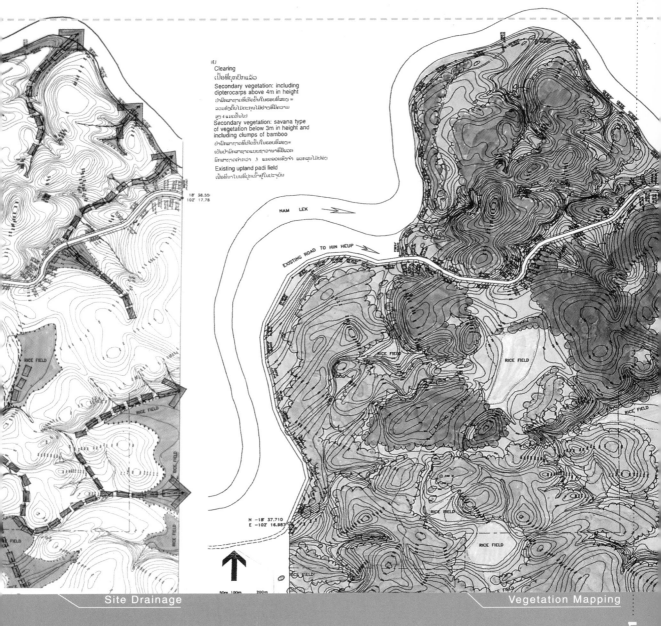

IEJ
Clearing
ເປົ່າທີ່ຖາງປ່າແລ້ວ

Secondary vegetation: including
dipterocarps above 4m in height
ປ່າມີພາຍຊາດທີ່ເປັນຢັ້ນໃນຮອບທີ່ສອງ =
ຄວມຕັ້ງຍື່ນໄມ້ຍະການໄມ້ປ່າງທີ່ມີຄວາມ
ສູງ 4 ແມໜ້ອຍໄປໃນ

Secondary vegetation: savana type
of vegetation below 3m in height and
including clumps of bamboo
ປ່າມີພາຍຊາດທີ່ເປັນຢັ້ນໃນຮອບທີ່ສອງ =
ເປັນປ່າມີພາຍຊາດແນວຊະວານາທີ່ມີພາຍ
ມີພາຍຊາດຕ່າກວ່າ 3 ແມຄວມຕັ້ງຈຳ ຄວມຊຸມໄມ້ປ່ອງ

Existing upland padi field
ເປົ່າທີ່ເກາໃບໜີ່ຖ້າເປັນຮູ້ຮູ້ປະຈຸບັນ

18° 58.55ı
102° 17.78

NAM   LEX

EXISTING ROAD TO HIN HEUP

N −18° 37.710
E −102° 16.987

RICE FIELD

RICE FIELD

RICE FIELD

RICE FIELD

RICE FIELD

RICE FIELD

RICE FIELD

RICE FIELD

50m 100m   200m

Site Drainage   Vegetation Mapping

gether with suggested venues for events in temple, hall, square or street, distributed within the township map.
The emphasis overall is once again, the groundscraper as a natural landscape form, with minimum impact and
maximum integration.

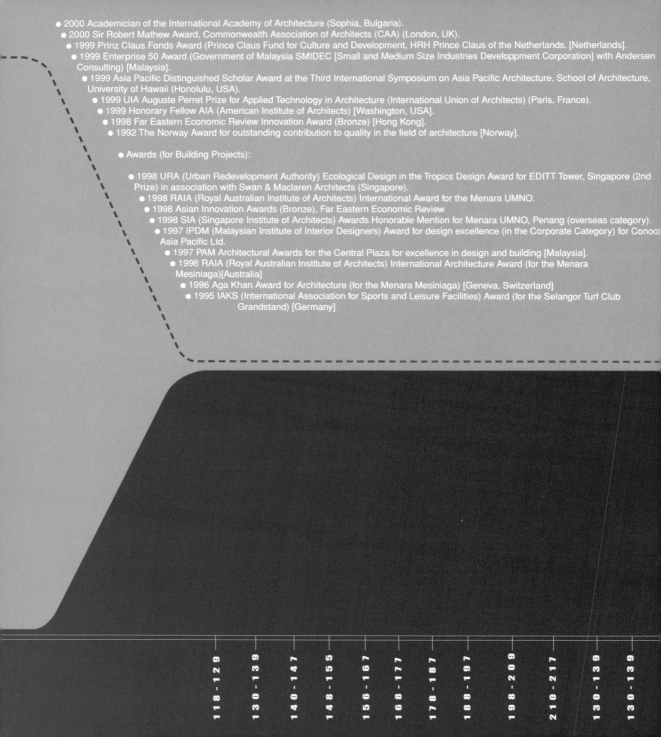

● 2000 Academician of the International Academy of Architecture (Sophia, Bulgaria).
● 2000 Sir Robert Mathew Award, Commonwealth Association of Architects (CAA) (London, UK).
● 1999 Prinz Claus Fonds Award (Prince Claus Fund for Culture and Development, HRH Prince Claus of the Netherlands. [Netherlands].
● 1999 Enterprise 50 Award (Government of Malaysia SMIDEC [Small and Medium Size Industries Developpment Corporation] with Andersen Consulting) [Malaysia].
● 1999 Asia Pacific Distinguished Scholar Award at the Third International Symposium on Asia Pacific Architecture, School of Architecture, University of Hawaii (Honolulu, USA).
● 1999 UIA Auguste Perret Prize for Applied Technology in Architecture (International Union of Architects) (Paris, France).
● 1999 Honorary Fellow AIA (American Institute of Architects) [Washington, USA].
● 1998 Far Eastern Economic Review Innovation Award (Bronze) [Hong Kong].
● 1992 The Norway Award for outstanding contribution to quality in the field of architecture [Norway].

● Awards (for Building Projects):

● 1998 URA (Urban Redevelopment Authority) Ecological Design in the Tropics Design Award for EDITT Tower, Singapore (2nd Prize) in association with Swan & Maclaren Architects (Singapore).
● 1998 RAIA (Royal Australian Institute of Architects) International Award for the Menara UMNO.
● 1998 Asian Innovation Awards (Bronze), Far Eastern Economic Review
● 1998 SIA (Singapore Institute of Architects) Awards Honorable Mention for Menara UMNO, Penang (overseas category).
● 1997 IPDM (Malaysian Institute of Interior Designers) Award for design excellence (in the Corporate Category) for Conoc Asia Pacific Ltd.
● 1997 PAM Architectural Awards for the Central Plaza for excellence in design and building [Malaysia].
● 1996 RAIA (Royal Australian Institute of Architects) International Architecture Award (for the Menara Mesiniaga)[Australia]
● 1996 Aga Khan Award for Architecture (for the Menara Mesiniaga) [Geneva, Switzerland]
● 1995 IAKS (International Association for Sports and Leisure Facilities) Award (for the Selangor Turf Club Grandstand) [Germany]

118 - 129   130 - 139   140 - 147   148 - 155   156 - 167   168 - 177   178 - 187   188 - 197   198 - 209   210 - 217   130 - 139   130 - 139

- 1995 IAKS (International Association for Sports and Leisure Facilities) Award (for the Selangor Turf Club Grandstand) [Germany]
- 1995 SIA (Singapore Institute of Architects) Design Award (Overseas Category), Honorary Mention (for the Selangor Turf Club Grandstand) (Singapore)
- 1995 Merit Award, Kenneth F.Brown Asia Pacific Culture and Architecture Design Award (for the Roof-Roof House) (Hawaii, USA)
- 1993 PAM Architecture Award for the Menara Mesiniaga for excellence in design for commercial buildings.[Malaysia]
- 1993 PAM Architecture Award (Honorary Mention) for Conservation (for the Standard Chartered Bank, Penang) [Malaysia]
- 1993 IATA (International Award for Innovative Technology in Architecture), Top 20 Finalist, Quaternario [Italy]
- 1993 2nd MSG/MSID (Malaysian Institute of Interior Designers) commercial interior and display design award for the Seacorp light-fittings.
- 1992 The Norway Award for outstanding contribution to quality in the field of architecture [Norway]
- 1991 PAM Architecture Award for commercial building. [Malaysia]
- 1991 PAM Architecture Award for single residential building (for the MS Tan House) [Malaysia]
- 1989 PAM Architectural Awards for the IBM Plaza for excellence in design and building [Malaysia]
- 1989 PAM Architectural Awards for The Weld Interior for excellence in design and building [Malaysia]
- 1989 Antron Design Award Honorable Mention [USA]
- 1988 Antron Design Award Honorable Mention [USA]
- 1987 Commonwealth Association of Architects (London) Commendation (for the book: "Tropical Verandah City") [London]

- Competition Prizes:

- 2001 Winning Entry, Enterprise 4, Singapore Institute of Architects - Hunter Douglas Design competition (Hypothetical Category), Singapore
- 2001 Winning Entry, Beijing World Science & Trade Centre, Beijing Municipal Institute of city Planning Design, China
- 2000 Winning Entry, Southwark Land Regeneration, Elephant & Castle, Southwark (Submission made jointly with others).
- 2000 Winning Entry, Tech-Linx Facilities Competition, Cyberjaya, Kuala Lumpur [Malaysia].
- 2000 Winning Entry, Huannan Masterplan Competition, Huanna, China for Hopsons International plc. (HK).
- 2000 Top Three Commendation Entry, "Living in the City" Competition. (Special Commendation).
- 1999 Winning Entry Singapore National Library, 2-stage Open Competition. (Submitted under Swan & Maclaren Architects), [Singapore].
- 1997 Winning Entry Subang Jaya Urban Center Masterplan, Selangor. Limited Competition [Malaysia].
- 1994 3rd Prize Entry Taichung Civic Centre & Town Hall, Taiwan, UIA International Open Competition [Taiwan].
- 1985 Citation Dewan Bandaraya Kuala Lumpur, Urban Design Open Competition, Kuala Lumpur City Hall, Kuala Lumpur [Malaysia].
- 1984 1st Prize Penang Swimming Club Masterplan and Extension Open Competition (in association with Laurence Loh Arkitek) Penang, [Malaysia].

- 1984 1st Prize Penang Swimming Club Masterplan and Extension Open Competition (in association with Laurence Loh Arkitek) Penang, [Malaysia].

awards

- France : "Beijing World Science & Trade Centre". Archilab a Orleans. (2001)
- London: in "Living in the City", Design Museum, London, UK (2000).
- London: "Expo 2005 Tower", Front Member's Room, AA School, London, (May 1998).
- East Berlin: "Energetics" (with Yeohlee), Aedes East Gallery, Berlin, (June 1998).
- Rotterdam: "Energetics" (with Yeohlee), Netherlands Institute of Architecture (NAI), Rotterdam, Netherlands, (September 1998).
- New York: "The Skyscraper, Bioclimatically Considered", in The Architectural League of New York, NYC, USA (January 1997).
- London: "Bioclimatic Skyscrapers" in Building Centre, London, (February 1995).
- Berlin: "Bioclimatic Skyscrapers" in Aedes West Gallery, Berlin, (1994).
- Tokyo: "Contemporary Architects Exhibition" in Nara Town Hall, Triennale Nara, Japan, (1992).
- Tokyo: "Tropical Skyscrapers" in Tokyo Designers Space Gallery, Axis Building, Tokyo, (January 1990).
- Tokyo: "Houses - 7 KL Architects" in Tokyo Ginza Pocket Park Gallery, Tokyo, (1985) (with six other architects).

'Energetics' - Aedes Gallery, East Berlin, 1998. A collaboration with Yeohlee, a Malaysian Fashion Designer based in New York

● Key Books, Monographs and Publications :

Yeang, K. (2000), The Green Skyscraper: The Basis for Designing Sustainable Intensive Buildings , Prestel, Munich, Germany
Yeang, K. (2000), Service Cores in Buildings, John Wiley & Sons, Ltd.
Yeang, K.(1997), The Skyscraper: Bioclimatically Considered: A Design Primer, Academy Group, Architectural Design, London. Reprinted 1999, John Wiley & Sons, London.
Yeang,K. (1995), Designing with Nature, McGraw-Hill, USA.
Yeang,K. (1992), The Architecture of Malaysia (1890-1990), Pepin Press, Holland (2nd Edition in preparation).
Yeang,K. (1987), Tropical Urban Regionalism, MIMAR, Singapore.
Yeang,K. (1986), Tropical Verandah City, Longman , Malaysia.
Yeang,K.(1981), PhD Dissertation: "A Theoretical Framework for the Incorporation of Ecological Considerations in the Design and Planning of the Built Environment", Cambridge University Library, England (Subsequently published as Yeang, K. (1995), Designing with Nature, McGraw-Hill, USA).
Yeang,K.(1974), "Bionics: The Use of Biological Analogies in Design", in AAQ No.4 (Architectural Association Quarterly).
Yeang,K.(1974), "The Energetics of the Built Environment", in Architectural Design, July, Architectural Press, London.
Yeang,K.(1972), "Bases for Ecosystem Design", in Architectural Design, July, Architectural Press.London.

The work of T. R. Hamzah & Yeang Sdn. Bhd. have been published extensively in most architectural journals (Architectural Review, Architectural Record, AJ, Building Design, etc.).

'**Energetics**' - Aedes Gallery, East Berlin, 1998. A collaboration with Yeohlee, a Malaysian Fashion Designer based in New York

'Salone Internazionale dell'Industrializzazione Edilizia 2000' - Bolognia, Italy, 2000. A construction and building technology exhibition.

'Archilab a Orleans' - France, 2001. Featuring T. R. Hamzah & Yeang's winning scheme of Beijing World Science & Trade Centre

'Archilab a Orleans' - France, 2001. Featuring T. R. Hamzah & Yeang's winning scheme of Beijing World Science & Trade Centre

Al-Hilali Complex Tower
Principal-in-charge: Dr. Ken Yeang
Project Architect: Seow Ji Nee
Design Architect: Ridzwa Fathan
Design Team: Dana Cupkova
C&S and M&E Engineers: Battle McCarthy Consulting Engineers (London)
Quantity Surveyor: Juru Ukur Bahan Malaysia (KL)

Al-Asima Shopping Village
Principal-in-charge: Dr. Ken Yeang
Project Architect: Andy Chong
Design Architects: Max Loh Hock Jin, Ridzwa Fathan
Project Team: Beng Hin, Kenneth Cheong, Shahrul Kamaruddin, Voon Quek Wah
C&S and M&E Engineers: Battle McCarthy Consulting Engineers (London)
Environmental Design Consultant: Battle McCarthy Consulting Engineers (London)
Quantity Surveyors: Davis Landgon & Seah (KL)

BB Park Roof Canopy
Principal-in-charge: Dr. Ken Yeang
Project Architect: Chong Voon Wee
Design Architects: Ridzwa Fathan, Fabian Jungbeck
Drafting: Loh Mun Chee, Yap Yow Kong

Beijing World Science & Trade Centre
Principal-in-charge: Dr. Ken Yeang
Project Architect: Andy Chong
Design Architects: Ridzwa Fathan, Kenneth Cheong
Design Team: Renee Lee, Shahrul Kamaruddin,
Amy Chong, Antony Ridgers, Angie Foong,
Beng Hin, Ng Chee Hui, Joris Tan,
Lena Ng

featured projects
& key members

Bishopsgate Towers (Mixed-use Residential)
Principal-in-charge: Dr. Ken Yeang
Project Architect: Andy Chong
Design Architects: Chuck Yeoh Thiam Yew, Jason Yeang
Project Team: Ridzwa Fathan, Gezin Andicen, Ong Eng Huat, Ooi Tee Lee, Loh Mun Chee
Project Engineer: Buro Happold (London)
Quantity Surveyor: Davis Langdon & Everest (London), David Langdon & Seah
Environmental Simulations: Total Building Performance Team, National University of Singapore

Business Advancement Technology Centre
Principal-in-charge: Dr. Ken Yeang
Project Architect: Tim Mellor
Design Architects: Ridzwa Fathan, Chuck Yeoh Thiam Yew, Sam Jacoby, Ravin Ponniah, James Douglas Gerwin

Enterprise Building 4
Principal-in-charge: Dr. Ken Yeang
Project Architect: Mohamad Pital Maarof
Design Architects: Ridzwa Fathan, Francis Hur
Design Team: Ong Eng Huat, Joris Tan Tien Shen

Hipa Township Masterplan
Principal-in-charge: Dr. Ken Yeang
Project Architect: Eddie K. L. Chan
Design Team: Yvonne Ho Wooi Lee
Project Team: Andrei Vouk, Yukiko Yakoo
Consultant: Michael Sorkin Studio

Hin Lim • Kirsten • Andy C • Ridzwa F • Frank •   Poh Lye Ooi   •   Aya Maeda   •   Alex Lei   • Shahrul Nizam • Lena Ng
Chee Hui   •Kevin Cheung•Ms. Voon•Chong Voon•Mr. Loh•Max •   Sze Tho kok Cheng • Sze Tho Kok Hooh   •   Amy Chong • K3

Town Planner: Simon Saw
C&S Engineers: Jurutera Konsultant (S) Sdn. Bhd. (Lam Kok Houp)
Model Maker: Technibuilt Sdn. Bhd.

Huanan New City Masterplan and Residential Township in Guangzhou, China
Principal-in-charge: Dr. Ken Yeang
Project Architect: Chong Voon Wee
Design Architects: Chuck Yeoh, Ridzwa Fathan, Jason Yeang
Project Team: Ong Eng Huat, Kenneth Cheong, Azril Amir Jaafar, Gezin Andicen, Loh Mun Chee, Margaret Ng, Mah Lek, Ooi Poh Lye, Yap Yow Kong, Rahimah Lasim, Sze Tho Kok Cheng, Voon Quek Wah
C&S and M&E Engineers: Buro Happold (M) Sdn. Bhd. (Malaysia)
Feng Shui Master: Jerry Too
Town Planner & Landscape Architect: Simon Saw
Quantity Surveyor: Levett & Bailey (Hong Kong & Guangzhou)

Jabal Omar Towers
Principal-in-charge: Dr. Ken Yeang
Project Architect: Andy Chong
Design Director: Ridzwa Fathan
Design Architects: Portia Reynolds, Kenneth Cheong
Design Team: Ong Eng Huat, Ng Chee Hui, Lena Ng, Peter Fajak, Max Loh Hock Jin, Shahrul Kamaruddin, Maulud Tawang, Wong Yee Wah, Celine Verissimo
Drafting: Mah Lek, Loh Mun Chee, Margaret Ng
C&S and M&E Engineers: Saudi Consulting Services (Riyadh)
Bioclimatic Consultants: Battle McCarthy Consulting Engineers (London), Dr. Error! Bookmark not defined. (California)
Perspectives Illustrator: Peter Edgeley (Melbourne)

Rajiv Ratnarajah   •   Kwai Hoong   •   Mohd Pital Maarof   •   Monie   •   K3   •   Shahrul   •   Chong Voon W
Tim Mellor   •   Lena Ng   •   Amy CJ Chong   •   Kirsten Karst   •   Lena Ng   •   Ridzwa Fathan   •   Andy Chong   •   Yee Seng Ta

Landscape Consultant: Simon Saw Landscape & Planning (KL)
Photography: K. L. Ng Photography
Model Maker: Technibuilt Sdn. Bhd.

Lake Club Extension Competition (unplaced)
Principal-in-charge: Dr. Ken Yeang
Project Architect: Goon Li Chin

Malaysia Design Technology Centre (MDTC)
Principal-in-charge: Dr. Ken Yeang
Project Architect: Alex Lei
Design Architect: Ridzwa Fathan
Assistant Architects: Ong Eng Huat, Renee Lee, Amy Chong Cheen Jian, Rohan s/o Gopa Kumar, Angeline Foong Yar Her, Mohammad Farris B. Baharom, Joris Tan Tien Shen
3-D Modelling: Francis Hur

Marsham Street Urban Design
Principal-in-charge: Dr. Ken Yeang
Design Architects: Paul Standford, Grace Tan, Mark Lucas, Strachan Forgan

Mewah-Oils Headquarters
Principal-in-charge: Dr. Ken Yeang
Project Architect: Chong Voon Wee
Design Architects: Max Loh Hock Jin, Ridzwa Fathan, Peter Fajak
Drafting: Mah Lek, Voon Quek Wah, Sze Tho Kok Cheng

Lena Ng • Kirsten Karst • Lena Ng • Amy Chong • Alex Lei • Joanne Tan
Angie Foong • Lena • Beng Hin • Max Loh • Shi Yi • Amy • K3 • Jane Lin • Renee Lee • Badieh

C&S Engineer: Rekanan Jurutera Perunding
M&E Engineer: Norman Disney & Young Sdn. Bhd.
Quantity Surveyor: JUB Padu
Landscape Architect: Simon Saw

Nottingham University in Malaysia Campus
Principal-in-charge: Dr. Ken Yeang
Project Architect: Andy Chong
Design Architects: Ridzwa Fathan, Jane Lin, Kenneth Cheong
Design Team: Ong Eng Huat, Lena Ng, Renee Lee, Antony Ridgers, Maulud Taufik, Shahrul Kamaruddin

PLA Western Redevelopment
Principal-in-charge: Dr. Ken Yeang
Project Architect: Anne-Laura Gimenez
Design Architects: Anne-Laura Gimenez, Portia Reynolds

SD Headquarters and Condominium
Principal-in-charge: Dr. Ken Yeang
Design Architect: Ridzwa Fathan
Project Team: Timothy Harold Wort, Keith Leong, Alun White, Strachan Forgan, Mark Lucas, Dana Cupkova

Tengku Robert Hamzah • Andy Chong • **Dr. Ken Yeang** • Ji Nee Seow • Ridzwa Fathan • Yeohlee • **Dr. Ken Yea**
Ridzwa Fathan•Tim Wort •Jorris Tan•Shahrul Nizam•Louise MacKenzie•Renee Lee•Tim Mellor•K3 • Frank Hur • Amy Chong • Yenniu Lim

Masterplan for Taipei Capital City
Principal-in-charge: Dr. Ken Yeang
Project Architect: Andy Chong
Design Architects: Ridzwa Fathan, Kenneth Cheong
Project Team: Beng Hin, Lena Ng, Francis Hur, Shahrul Kamaruddin
Local Architect & Landscape Consultant: Yu Ming Kuo & Associates (Taipei)
Feng Shui Consultant: Master Jerry Too

Tech-Linx Technology Park
Principal-in-charge: Dr. Ken Yeang
Project Architect: Neil Harris
Design Director: Ridzwa Fathan
Design Architects: Kenneth Cheong (Key Design Areas), Tim Mellor (Canopy & Curtain Wall), Portia Reynolds (Internal Layouts)
Technical & Drawings: Rajiv Ratnarajah
Project Team: Yap Yow Kong, Voon Quek Wah, Kevin Chung, Choo Poo Liang, Lena Ng, Shahrul Kamaruddin, Maulud bin Tawang

Telekom Multimedia University Masterplan
Principal-in-charge: Dr. Ken Yeang
Project Architect: Azri Razif Bin Yahaya
Design Architect: Ridzwa Fathan
Project Team: Chuck Yeoh Thiam Yew, Sam Jacoby, Tim Wort, Anne-Laura Gimenez
Quantity Surveyor: Juru Ukur Bahan Malaysia (Ong See Lian)
Landscape Architect: Aspinwall Clouston (Robert van Noujuys)
Town Planner: Planning & Development Consultant (Simon Saw)

ra Giminez • Ridzwa Fathan • Sam Jacoby   • Yenniu Lim • Ridzwa Fathan • Andrew • Yvonne Ho • Eng Huat Ong • Azman Che Mat • Azril • EHT
y • Janet Yue • Lian See Quaik • Frank Hur•Tim Mellor•Beng Hin•Anthony Ridgers•Rajiv•Renee•Frank•Kate Butler•K3•   Shahrul Nizam

Tianjin Civil Aviation School
Principal-in-charge: Dr. Ken Yeang
Project Architect: Yvonne Ho Wooi Lee
Design Architects: Yvonne Ho Wooi Lee, Ridzwa Fathan
Design Development Architects: James Douglas Gerwin, Mohd Azman Che Mat

Urban Design for the Er Mei Street in the old Theatre District, Taipei
Principal-in-charge: Dr. Ken Yeang
Project Architect: Stephanie Lee Shu Mei
Design Architects: Ridzwa Fathan, Ong Eng Huat, Gezin Anderson
Model Maker: Technibuilt Sdn Bhd

Wanliu Park Masterplan
Principal-in-charge: Dr. Ken Yeang
Project Architect: Alex Lei
Design Architect: Yvonne Ho Wooi Lee
Assistant Architects: Lena Ng, Ng Chee Hui, Renee Lee
Drafting: Margaret Ng
C&S Engineers: SRSB Jurutera Perunding Sdn. Bhd.
M&E Engineers: Norman Disney & Young Sdn. Bhd.
Landscape Architect: Simon Saw
Feng Shui Master: Jerry Too Life-Secret Fortune

Mah Lek • Mr. Yap • Miss Voon • Kevin Cheung • Mr. Loh • Max Loh • Lay Lay • Irene Ching • Loo See Che
Margaret Ng • Mohani Mohariff • Alex Lei • Beng Hin • Kirsten Karst • Andy Chong • Kenneth Che

WIPO – Proposed Extension of World Intellectual Administrative Headquarters
Principal-in-charge: Dr. Ken Yeang
Project Architect: Chong Voon Wee
Design Architects: Ridzwa Fathan, Astrid Schneider, Max Loh Hock Jin, Gezin Andicen, Ong Eng Huat

.ay Yeoh • Yee Seng • Shanmuganathan • Aya Maeda • Kevin Chung • Ooi • Loh • Chee Hui • Voon Quek Wah • Rahimah Lasim
A Harris • Beng Hin Lim • Kirsten B Karst • Ooi Poh Lye • Chee Hui Ng • Loh Mun Chee • Lian See Quaik • Loo See Chew

credits

Cover Design
Ridzwa A Fathan + Yenniu Lim

Concept
Ridzwa A Fathan

Graphic Design
Yenniu Lim

Pagelayout
Yenniu Lim with the assisstance of Francis Hur, Shahrul Nizam, Amy CJ Chong and Lena Ng

Illustration for Diagrams + Plans + Elevations + Sections
FrancisHur, Aya Maeda, Kirsten B Karst, Shahrul Nizam, Yee Seng Tan, Amy CJ Chong, Lena Ng, Yenniu Lim

3D Modelling
Shahrul Nizam, Francis Hur, Ridzwa A Fathan

Material Compilation
Yenniu Lim with the assistance of Aman Krishan, Rita Yen Chun Lee, Antonia Josten, Aman Krishan

Annotation + Labelling
Andy Chong, Kirsten B Karst, Aya Maeda, Yee Seng Tan, Yenniu Lim

Printing + Binding
EHT Creative & Graphic Services

Contact
8 Jalan 1, Taman Sri Ukay, Off Jalan Ulu Klang, 68 000, Ampang, Selangor, Malaysia
[tel. no.] 00 603 2357 1966 [fax no.] 00 603 4256 1005
[email address] trhy@tm.net.my

Website
www.trhamzahyeang.com

© T. R. Hamzah & Yeang Sdn. Bhd